SpringerBriefs in Criminology

SpringerBriefs in Criminology present concise summaries of cutting edge research across the fields of Criminology and Criminal Justice. It publishes small but impactful volumes of between 50-125 pages, with a clearly defined focus. The series covers a broad range of Criminology research from experimental design and methods, to brief reports and regional studies, to policy-related applications.

The scope of the series spans the whole field of Criminology and Criminal Justice, with an aim to be on the leading edge and continue to advance research. The series will be international and cross-disciplinary, including a broad array of topics, including juvenile delinquency, policing, crime prevention, terrorism research, crime and place, quantitative methods, experimental research in criminology, research design and analysis, forensic science, crime prevention, victimology, criminal justice systems, psychology of law, and explanations for criminal behavior.

SpringerBriefs in Criminology will be of interest to a broad range of researchers and practitioners working in Criminology and Criminal Justice Research and in related academic fields such as Sociology, Psychology, Public Health, Economics and Political Science.

Ílison Dias Dos Santos

Aporophobia and Punitive Power in Brazil

Guidelines for a Failed Critical-Criminological Concept

Springer

Ílison Dias Dos Santos
University of Barcelona
Barcelona, Spain

ISSN 2192-8533 ISSN 2192-8541 (electronic)
SpringerBriefs in Criminology
ISBN 978-3-032-01752-9 ISBN 978-3-032-01753-6 (eBook)
https://doi.org/10.1007/978-3-032-01753-6

Translation from the Portuguese language edition: "Aporofobia e poder punitivo no brasil lineamentos de um conceito criminológico-crítico frustrado" by Ílison Dias Dos Santos, © Ílison Dias dos Santos 2020. Published by Universidade Federal da Bahia. All Rights Reserved.

The original submitted manuscript has been translated into English. The translation was done using artificial intelligence. A subsequent revision was performed by the author(s) to further refine the work and to ensure that the translation is appropriate concerning content and scientific correctness. It may, however, read stylistically different from a conventional translation.

This Springer imprint is published by the registered company Springer Nature Switzerland AG
The registered company address is: Gewerbestrasse 11, 6330 Cham, Switzerland

"There is an urgent need to act if we truly want to integrate Brazilian society, so that, in the near future, being Black in Brazil will also mean being fully Brazilian in Brazil."[1]

---

[1] Santos, M. (2002). *O país distorcido: O Brasil, a globalização e a cidadania*. São Paulo: Publifolha, p. 161.

To Leandro Encarnação da Mata, my beloved father, the guide of my Orí

Foreword

Paradoxes abound in today's world, particularly in the realm of criminal justice. This essay explores aporophobia in two ways—or, more precisely, as a concept with two attributed functions: on the one hand, as a critical lens through which to analyze the exercise of punitive power; on the other hand, as a qualifying factor within certain criminal classifications.

With regard to the first function, it is important to note that criminal law—that is, the program of primary criminalization, or its normative *ought-to-be*—does not appear to be discriminatory, at least not in any overt way. However, upon closer analysis, elements of a discriminatory nature can be identified.

Penal law, however, enables the exercise of a highly discriminatory formal punitive power—one that also tolerates another kind of power: the informal, which, according to the same law, is criminal. The combined effect of formal and informal punitive power—legal and illegal alike—can be seen in the composition of the prison population and in police lethality. It is undeniable that the majority of those imprisoned and killed are, predominantly, poor people.

This fact, observable across the globe, is not enough, however, to explain criminalizing selection. After all, the poor and the precarious make up the majority of the population in our América. If selection truly obeyed class alone, it would function by pure chance—a kind of lottery among the many. But everything suggests that this is not the case.

In reality, the selection of those who are incarcerated—and of the victims of the executive agencies of the penal apparatus—is based on how closely they conform to certain stereotypes constructed by the media. As the author of this critical essay rightly observes, it is not only poverty that plays a part, but these representations are also nourished by all the reasons for discrimination supplied by the full array of each society's most deeply rooted and vile prejudices.

Without even resorting to the statistics mentioned here, it is enough to visit any prison in Brazil to witness the overwhelming presence of melanin that dominates its population. Undeniably, they are poor—but, as the author rightly notes, they are poor Black and Brown people. This selection is also facilitated by the fact that these individuals tend to commit rudimentary crimes—crimes that are easily detectable, given their lack of training for more sophisticated offenses. Meanwhile, those with greater resources and less melanin, besides not matching the prevailing stereotype, are more likely to commit discreet crimes, made possible by their broader technical repertoire.

My country, Argentina, does not bear the same scar of slavery as Brazil—if only because, due to climatic conditions, we never had the kind of intensive plantations that could sustain such an economy. However, this does not mean that racist prejudices and other forms of discrimination are absent from Argentine society.

Our prisons, too, are filled with low-income individuals—not solely because of their class condition, but because they also embody the other discriminatory traits that feed the stereotype of the Argentine delinquent: residents of peripheral neighborhoods, youth, those who wear certain kinds of clothing, the poorly or uneducated, immigrants from neighboring countries, sex workers, and so on.

It is, therefore, quite naive to attempt a critique of criminalizing and incarcerating selectivity based solely on a country's poverty line. Nor can one claim that such stereotyped selection always stems from an overt feeling of hatred—much less from a clear-cut phobia. The bureaucratic ease with which these populations are targeted must not be overlooked, especially given the rudimentary nature of their offenses, which makes them easily detectable by the police bureaucracy. Nor should we underestimate a certain degree of fear in the face of a growing majority—one that, if united through solidarity, organization, and collective action, could pose a threat to established power structures.

The geopolitically subordinate position of the countries in our region leads to the periodic regression of the Rule of Law, driven by the proconsuls of transnational interests who hold power in our republics—once through genocidal dictatorships, and now through the chaos of fragile democracies. These regressions, cloaked in the ideology known as *neoliberalism*, dismantle even the most modest efforts toward a *Welfare State* or collective well-being. As unmet needs grow, they give rise to a *State of Discomfort*—an anti-welfare state—that strengthens the repressive apparatus, turning society as a whole into a prison. This is what we now witness in Argentina, where not only the stereotyped are incarcerated, but also political opponents and dissidents, through lawfare and sheer police abuse.

Aporophobia, far from being an explanation for the selectivity of punitive power, is itself a feeling fueled by the ideology of the proconsuls of contemporary colonialism—nothing more, in the end, than a renewal of old *Spencerianism*. The anthropological logic merely shifts from biological to economic reductionism: the former "animal," whose brain had allegedly not yet reached the developmental level of the colonizers and thus had to disappear so the strongest and most evolved could reproduce, is now replaced by the poor, who are always seen as inferior not by nature, but by failure in the meritocratic struggle for economic success—an unfitness that must not disturb the *homo economicus*, who moves through all dimensions of life governed by the laws of supply and demand, and who achieves success solely through individual effort.

It must be clear that we cannot confuse fundamentally different levels of analysis. Criticizing the aporophobic component of so-called neoliberal ideology is one thing, but it is quite another to believe that aporophobia alone is the key to explaining secondary criminalizing selection. Poverty is merely one among many components that feed the stereotype through which processes of selection and labeling are carried out.

The second meaning or function attributed to the concept of aporophobia is its use as a possible qualifying circumstance to aggravate penalties in certain crimes—especially homicide. The paradox lies in the fact that the very power structures that ideologically promote aporophobia also attempt to invoke it in order to increase punishment for crimes against life or physical integrity, when such crimes are motivated by that same bias.

Although there are indeed cases of homicides and assaults committed against people without means—particularly those living on the streets of our cities—motivated by nothing other than the desire to harm them, I believe such crimes are already covered under the category of those aggravated by a trivial motive. Thus, by attempting to classify them once again in a distinct way, we run the risk of implying that, in these cases, the law does not recognize the motive as trivial. In any case, as the author of this critical essay rightly observes, this would amount to an expression of symbolic criminal law, which, in our view, remains relatively harmless.

Buenos Aires, October 19, 2024

E. Raúl Zaffaroni
Emeritus Professor
University of Buenos Aires

Preface

This critical essay offers an overview of the deployment of the idea of aporophobia as a concept within critical criminology. It does not aim to be exhaustive, much less to offer the final word on the matter. What we seek, rather, is to trace the contours of a theoretical path—one that may offer meaningful heuristic tools for critical reflection on the subject.

For a long time, philosophers have understood that the first step—and perhaps the most important—in any theoretical endeavor is the proper formulation of questions. After all, poorly framed questions inevitably lead to partially or entirely flawed answers. It is the questions, ultimately, that shape the kind of response one seeks to draw from reality—and also determine which aspects, voluntarily or otherwise, one chooses to leave in the shadows.

This is precisely what we aim to construct in this essay: questions that cast light on the subject. To that end, we highlight some of the key problems raised by the topic, as we have chosen to frame it. Naturally, we do not claim to exhaust all of its complexities—nor do we believe that the current state of the art allows for definitive conclusions. Rather, we propose a few non-definitive conclusions, necessary steps to further the ongoing reflection on the matter.

Finally, I would like to express my thanks—with the *cri du cœur* that defines us—to the colleagues who insisted, almost tirelessly, that we publish this critical essay. Originally written some years ago for a particular moment in academic life, it has, in their view, not lost its relevance or urgency. Except for a few minor adjustments, the text remains faithful to the original version.

Barcelona, Spain
March 22, 2025

Ílison Dias Dos Santos

Competing Interests The author has no competing interests to declare that are relevant to the content of this manuscript.

Contents

Chapter 1
Introduction: The Invisibilization of the Part by the Whole

The prevailing idea seems to be that any critical formulation of punitive power carries, intrinsically, an emancipatory dimension. This line of thought has taken on the status of a kind of common sense—meant here without any negative connotation—in which every critique of the status quo is presumed to be valuable for its delegitimizing effect.

It so happens that in so-called complex problems[1]—as is undoubtedly the case with criminal issues—every critical perspective carries with it sensitive intrinsic and extrinsic elements that only come to light when the intended critique enters into dialog with the sociopolitical world that surrounds it.

Such a revealing dialog can only be undertaken from a perspective that is, at the very least, interdisciplinary—one that grasps the phenomenal characteristics of the empirical world which the critique seeks to engage.

This theoretical-methodological path becomes essential for anyone intending to engage in such critique—lest it end up justifying precisely what it feared most: the very oppression it claims to resist. In other words, criticism detached from local analysis is not only devoid of delegitimizing power; it ultimately functions as a legitimizing instrument for what, at least in theory, it set out to challenge.

Whether consciously or not, advocating a critical perspective on punitive power opens a series of theoretical windows that must be examined with care and precision. In some theoretical currents, such criticisms are deliberately shaped to camouflage their true objectives. This means that what often presents itself as revolutionary and critical may hide, through action or omission, the legitimization of what is being criticized.

We are not referring here to some elaborate conspiracy theories in which one deliberately chooses to camouflage theoretical—and, of course, political—interests beneath supposedly critical perspectives. Rather, what is at stake is a misunderstanding of the object of study in its full complexity and a denial of the field as an essential component of critique itself—one that necessarily demands a specific, situated, and local analysis.

Í. Dias Dos Santos, *Aporophobia and Punitive Power in Brazil*,
SpringerBriefs in Criminology,
https://doi.org/10.1007/978-3-032-01753-6_1

It is, then, a critique that stands in opposition to thought rooted in—and directed toward—a specific reality, as a presumption of the epistemological adequacy of the political act of criticizing.

When critique does not follow analysis—when it disregards the phenomenological context inherent to what it seeks to denounce—it gives rise to a kind of half-critique. In truth, a critique separated from analysis is not critique at all, even by etymological standards. The word *critique* comes from the Greek *krínein*, which means "to separate," "to distinguish"—in other words, critique means the analysis of something.[2]

The impulse to be critical merely for the sake of innovation ends up legitimizing a form of superficial critique—one that focuses on the effects of what is being criticized while almost entirely neglecting its underlying causes. This, in turn, contributes to the very reproduction and legitimization of the object in question. After all, in any cause-and-effect relationship, if I do not separate, distinguish, and neutralize the causes, the effects will persist.

To analyze these causes, the gaze must be local. Even when their origins are external, they materialize within a specific social reality—one that cannot be excluded from the gaze of any observer who aspires to be truly critical. Anything less would amount to, at best, a partial vision, and, like all partiality, it would produce outcomes quite different from those intended. It would resemble, in a way, the old legal-penal dichotomy between the *latent* and the *manifest*.

One of the most common pathways to this kind of partial critique is the tactic of making the part invisible through the whole. This consists of adopting a general critical premise—almost always true, incidentally—as a totalizing theoretical argument that ends up obscuring the actual origins or causes of the problem under study. Often, this happens unconsciously due to the absence of a local and interdisciplinary perspective on the object.

What is essentially lacking is an understanding of what precisely sustains such general critical premises. These are never nourished in the same way across all societies and latitudes,[3] for each society possesses its own idiosyncrasies—its specific social and political features—that shape the inequalities that define it. Indeed, it is these peculiarities that constitute the matrix through which some societies become more unequal than others.

This tactic is employed, for instance, when it is claimed that the underrepresentation of Black people in public higher education is essentially a matter of social class—supposedly having little or nothing to do with the structural racism that permeates Brazilian society. The argument goes: The problem is one of class, not race.

With this totalizing argument—that affirmative action policies, such as university quotas, should be based on income rather than race, as if poverty in Brazil were not deeply fueled by racism against Black and Brown people—the attempt is, first and foremost, to relocate the solution to this social problem into something generic and universal. That is, into something far more difficult to resolve—or into the realm of a kind of "revolution of the future," a revolution that, conveniently, no one knows exactly when (or if) it will arrive.

As Boaventura de Sousa Santos reminds us, in his classic empirical research on Brazilian social reality, "given the minimal political importance assigned to the issue of social inequalities, especially in Brazil [. . .], the idea of class racism becomes a way of disqualifying racism as a present and significant social phenomenon."[4]

It is obvious that we face a class problem. However, in Brazil, this problem is fundamentally fueled by structural—and structuring—racism. Emphasizing the class element alone does nothing but obscure what is most characteristic of our political, social, and legal structures: racism.

In other words, the analysis that precedes critique is not only essential—it must also be attentive to the local particularities of each society. This is especially true when engaging in the analysis and critique of the complex nature of punitive power in peripheral societies like our own.

In summary, we might say that the unforgettable words of Milton Santos apply perfectly here, as he reminds us that "when critique is not accompanied by analysis, it allows for mobilization, but not construction." The master from Bahia—of so many *Santos*—continues in the same captivating tone, stating: "critique should follow analysis, but in most cases, the need to be critical operates as if the analytical were dispensable. This is a factor of delay."[5]

From this perspective, we contend that the current trend of criticizing punitive power through the lens of aporophobia—understood as "the phobia of the poor that leads to the rejection of people, races, and ethnic groups that typically lack resources"[6]—does not, in itself, offer heuristic tools capable of capturing the complexity of punitive power in Brazil.

This philosophical concept, imported from another latitude—where punitive power operates under different conditions[7]—overlooks the central feature of how punitive power functions in Brazil: its slaveholding matrix, which has shaped the country's political, social, and legal institutions, along with other peculiarities of its enforcement. In Brazil, this matrix has remained a dominant structure "since the abolition of slavery, with which it was never effectively broken."[8]

Thus, if we insist on adopting the idea of aporophobia as conceived in the Global North—as a kind of literal and forced translation into our own peculiar reality—we risk producing a generalized *critique of everything*, one that ultimately contributes to legitimizing the current, unchecked exercise of punitive power. This happens through the invisibilization of the true structures that feed it. The result, inevitably, would be inadequate responses, since we would be starting from imported premises that are, without a doubt, ill-suited to our context.

In this sense, the present work seeks to offer a critical perspective on the application of the concept of aporophobia to our societal reality. It aims to demonstrate, in particular, how this concept may contribute to legitimizing punitive power by neglecting the specific dynamics that sustain its exercise in Brazil. It also highlights how such use represents a kind of importation—and literal translation—of a theory developed for other criminological realities, which is, in significant ways, incompatible with our own.

1.1 Theoretical-Methodological Option

There are many methodological paths one might take when approaching a scientific problem such as this. The choice of path reflects an analysis of which itinerary appears most appropriate in light of the characteristics and complexity of the object of study.

Similarly, the researcher's ideological and political preconceptions—since no one ever begins from a place of absolute neutrality—directly influence the choice of analytical method. For this reason, it is always a theoretical-methodological decision.[9] This is all the more evident in the field of the social sciences, to which criminal law and criminology belong.

In this sense, the scientific labor of our time is no longer compatible with explanations of social reality that treat social facts as "things in the world, considering social phenomena isolated from social manifestations."[10] Today, the most suitable approach acknowledges the need to analyze social phenomena in their interrelation, with the aim of apprehending them in a more complete way. Any micro-sociological reality can only be grasped through the interplay of non-hierarchical forms of knowledge—what might be called an "ecology of knowledge"[11]—capable of addressing the complexity of hypermodern problems.

As a logical consequence, the methodological path of this investigation is interdisciplinarity. This approach proves appropriate given the complexity of the object of study, offering a suitable framework to critically and reflectively illuminate the idea of aporophobia in relation to the exercise of punitive power in Brazil. No other theoretical-methodological choice would be coherent, since any critical analysis—like the one we pursue here—necessarily presupposes a method that is equally critical and inquisitive, distinct from the traditional dogmatic method of criminal science,[12] if the aim is truly to engage in a transformative critique.

It is precisely through this interrelation between disciplines that analysis gains depth, revealing the unprecedented and contributing to the ongoing advancement of scientific knowledge in our field of study.[13] It is in this sense that, today more than ever, the legal-criminal phenomenon, as a whole, cannot be understood apart from the idea that it is a "complex, social, and political problem, as well as an interdisciplinary one"[14]—which is precisely the methodological path we intend to follow in this investigation.

Notes

1. On the epistemological conception of so-called complex thinking, characteristic of socio-referenced academic work, see: Morin, E. (2005). *Introduction à la pensée complexe*. Paris: Éditions du Seuil, p. 15 ff.
2. Carpio, A. (2015). *Principios de filosofía*. Buenos Aires: Paidós, p. 83.
3. Zaffaroni, R. & Dias Dos Santos, Í. (2019). *La nueva crítica criminológica: Criminología en tiempos de totalitarismo financiero*. Buenos Aires: Ediar, p. 55 ff.

4. Sousa Santos, B. (2014). *O direito dos oprimidos*. Coimbra: Edições Almedina, p. 299.
5. Santos, M. (2007). *Encontros*. Rio de Janeiro: Beco do Azougue Editorial, p. 67.
6. Cortina, A. (2017). *Aporofobia, el rechazo al pobre*. Barcelona: Espasa Libros, p. 21.
7. Basoco, J. M. T. (2020). *Aporofobia y plutofilia: la deriva jánica de la política criminal contemporánea*. Barcelona: Bosch Editor, p. 14 ff.
8. Flauzina, A. L. P. (2017). *Corpo negro caído no chão: o sistema penal e o projeto genocida do Estado brasileiro*. Brasília: Brado Negro, p. 147.
9. Dias Dos Santos, Í. (2025). *En busca de la justicia restaurativa: un cambio de paradigma en el derecho penal de garantías* (2ª ed.). Buenos Aires: BdeF, p. 3.
10. Durkheim, É. (2007). *As regras do método sociológico*. São Paulo: Martins Fontes, p. 46.
11. Sousa Santos, B. & Almeida-Filho, N. (2008). *A universidade no século XXI: Para uma universidade nova*. Coimbra: Almedina, p. 69.
12. Gimbernat Ordeig, E. (1999). *Concepto y método de la ciencia del derecho penal*. Madrid: Tecnos, p. 13 ff.
13. Petrocelli, B. (1952). *Saggi di Diritto Penale*. Padova: CEDAM, p. 13.
14. Zúñiga Rodríguez, L. (2018). *Proyecto docente e investigador presentado en cumplimiento de la normativa vigente relativa al concurso a plaza de Catedrática de Derecho penal de la Universidad de Salamanca*. Salamanca: Universidad de Salamanca, p. 31.

Bibliography

Basoco, J. M. T. (2020). *Aporofobia y plutofilia: la deriva jánica de la política criminal contemporánea*. Bosch Editor.

Carpio, A. (2015). *Principios de filosofía*. Paidós.

Cortina, A. (2017). *Aporofobia, el rechazo al pobre*. Espasa Libros.

Dias Dos Santos, Í. (2025). *En busca de la justicia restaurativa: un cambio de paradigma en el derecho penal de garantías* (2ª ed.). BdeF.

Durkheim, É. (2007). *As regras do método sociológico*. Martins Fontes.

Flauzina, A. L. P. (2017). *Corpo negro caído no chão: o sistema penal e o projeto genocida do estado brasileiro*. Brado Negro.

Gimbernat Ordeig, E. (1999). *Concepto y método de la ciencia del derecho penal*. Tecnos.

Morin, E. (2005). *Introduction à la pensée complexe*. Éditions du Seuil.

Petrocelli, B. (1952). *Saggi di Diritto Penale*. CEDAM.

Santos, M. (2002). *O país distorcido: O Brasil, a globalização e a cidadania*. Publifolha.

Santos, M. (2007). *Encontros*. Beco do Azougue Editorial.

Sousa Santos, B. (2014). *O direito dos oprimidos*. Edições Almedina.

Sousa Santos, B. D., & Almeida-Filho, N. (2008). *A universidade no século XXI: Para uma universidade nova*. Almedina.

Zaffaroni, R., & Dias Dos Santos, Í. (2019). *La nueva crítica criminológica: criminología en tiempos de totalitarismo financiero*. Ediar.

Zúñiga Rodríguez, L. (2018). *proyecto docente e investigador presentado en cumplimiento de la normativa vigente relativa al concurso a plaza de Catedrática de Derecho penal de la Universidad de Salamanca*. Universidad de Salamanca.

Chapter 2
When Analysis Does Not Precede Criticism

2.1 Aporophobia as Brazilianophobia

The idea of aporophobia presents itself as a philosophically open concept—one that seeks to operate as a totalizing aphorism, a kind of hermeneutic key for the interpretation and critique of countless hypercomplex social phenomena, such as those relating to punitive power.

However, the historical experience of the lifeworld warns us of the dangers of singular critiques applied to complex problems, highlighting that what explains everything ultimately explains nothing.

It is not a matter of denying the hatred of the poor—or rather, of stereotyped vulnerable people—as a historically present and growing social phenomenon, especially in times of financial totalitarianism.[1] It is evident that aporophobia exists as a broad social phenomenon, largely driven by media monopolies in our late-colonized region.

The Brazilian elites, for example, have historically been characterized by their fear of the popular classes, systematically boycotting any and all national development projects aimed at income redistribution and the expansion of substantive citizenship[2]—projects capable of softening the dividing lines between rich and poor in the country.

This occurred with Getúlio's laborism, brought to an end by his suicide—practically induced; later, with the reforms proposed by João Goulart, violently interrupted by the 1964 coup; and, more recently, with the reactionary turn of the far right, which—supported by local elites—put an end to more than a decade of social inclusion policies.[3]

All of this has always been marked by a resentment—almost visceral—on the part of these elites, who have never made an effort to conceal it. And when they do, it is invariably in a crude and caricatured manner, resorting to folkloric elements such as the supposed fear of the return of communism—

Í. Dias Dos Santos, *Aporophobia and Punitive Power in Brazil*,
SpringerBriefs in Criminology,
https://doi.org/10.1007/978-3-032-01753-6_2

which, in truth, never existed as such in Brazil—a ridiculous return of what never was.

Notwithstanding all this, it is necessary to understand what explains this phenomenon—that is, *from which historical, social, and political matrix, the supposed aporophobia draws its strength*. This matrix is particular to each context: Every geopolitical space has its own engine of inequality[4] and, consequently, its own expression of punitive power, which *can only be critically examined in a localized and specific manner*.

Aporophobia is, so to speak, the macrosocial consequence of prior social processes—historically constructed and sustained by a whole sensitive microsocial fabric that must be unveiled if we truly want to solve it.

To understand the true causes behind the exercise of punitive power—both in general and, more specifically, in Brazil—it is essential to recognize that each country, even when sharing a regional context, possesses its own particular matrix that feeds the selective dynamics of punitive power.

Grounding a critique of a specific punitive reality on generalist elements such as poverty, inequality, social exclusion, discrimination, and now the so-called aporophobia—which, in some way, attempts to merge all these dimensions—is to contribute to the invisibilization of the actual forces that fuel it. It is, ultimately, to obscure the fact that from each geopolitical space emerges a distinct political-criminal dynamic in relation to the exercise—be it controlled or uncontrolled—of punitive power.

It also disregards the basic premise that every struggle requires specific weapons—just as it would make little sense to wage a battle in the Atlantic using war tanks. The same applies in the theoretical-methodological field: The tools employed must be compatible with the terrain; they must carry heuristic strength that responds to concrete problems, and, thus, they must be just as specific.

It is not a matter of proposing a specific science for each place. Naturally, what is scientifically conceived in other latitudes can serve to analyze problems elsewhere, since the laws of science—including those of the social sciences—are universal.

However, these same laws presuppose an ontological reality. The fact that poverty in Brazil is fueled by structural racism does not invalidate these laws, but it does demand that what is conceived as critical to punitive power in other contexts necessarily incorporates this dimension of our reality—otherwise, it risks producing sterile criticism or, worse, legitimizing what it purports to critique through invisibilization.

This kind of critique-of-everything ends up acting as a disorganizing force against resistance itself, as it disregards, among other things, the specificities of each struggle—its layers, its epistemic crossroads, and its moments of encounter and disconnection. Poverty, for instance, is not embodied in the same way across all vulnerable bodies. To be poor and white in Brazil is one thing; to be poor and Black—which, according to statistics, is the general rule—is quite another, especially given that, in our tropical margin, these categories almost always overlap, with the former feeding upon the latter.

The stereotype also plays a crucial role here,[5] ultimately determining—through secondary criminalization—the targets of criminalizing and victimizing selection, even when that stereotype is fictitiously constructed by media oligopolies that exploit Brazil's deeply rooted racial prejudices. All of this occurs with the indispensable—and perennial—collaboration of the state, which "formulates, corroborates, and implements a discourse and policies portraying Black individuals as subjects to be feared and, therefore, to be repressed. Society, permeated by fear through this discourse and ideological background, corroborates and encourages violence, torture, imprisonment, and genocide."[6]

Thus, Black and Brown individuals are those who embody the figure of the violent delinquent—the social pariah constructed by the media[7]—who provokes fear when walking down a quiet street; who makes people clutch their bags more tightly when sitting next to them on public transport; who are humiliated when trying to enter bank branches with their revolving doors; and who must carry as many documents as possible each day in case of a police search—situations in which they are forced to prove they are not criminals, despite being Black or Brown.

Understanding these specificities that feed the selectivity of our punitive power is essential for the construction of any criticism that aspires to liberation. To deny this is not only epistemologically flawed but also works to block any potential for collective organization aimed at overcoming this selective violence. Worse still, it leaves unchallenged the idea that the disorganization of the oppressed, as an empowered social class, is somehow their own fault.

When the diversity of resistance itself is disregarded—and the fact that it must be seen and understood as such—their lack of organization is often attributed to a lack of political consciousness, a lack of group identity, or a long list of other supposed deficiencies.[8]

In addition, the notion of aporophobia fosters a certain socially normalizing conformity, since virtually the entire capitalist world—especially in this era of financial totalitarianism—is immersed in social problems related to poverty and inequality. There is no need to assume any particular negative protagonism before the world or oneself when recognizing the existence of an *aporophobic criminal law*.[9] In fact, criminal law has always been aporophobic.

Framing the idea that we live in an aporophobic society or under an aporophobic punitive power as a hermeneutic premise does not generate, in the same proportion, the kind of social disapproval provoked by, for instance, the circumstantiated premise that a society operates under a racist or xenophobic punitive power.

Given the minimal political relevance that inequality has acquired in the era of financial capitalism—where it is viewed as structural and inevitable—focusing on aporophobia ends up invisibilizing the truly meaningful struggles for transformation, such as those against racism, xenophobia, misogyny, homophobia, and others. These struggles are either seen as socially irrelevant phenomena or, at best, relegated to marginal status, stripping them of their true political significance.

This critical perspective on the idea of aporophobia as linked to punitive power seems to us valid not only for our Brazilian and Latin American margins. Nor do we believe that the problem of punitive power in Spain—the country of origin of the notion of aporophobia, both in general and as a criminological concept—can be explained by the exercise of an aporophobic criminal law, despite the excessive imprisonment of immigrants for property crimes and incarceration rates that are incompatible with the country's low levels of violence.[10]

Even there, aporophobia, when understood as a criminological-critical concept, acts as a mechanism of invisibilization of the actual sociopolitical matrix that fuels the selectivity of its punitive power. When it is claimed, for example, that Spanish criminal law is aporophobic and that aggressions against homeless individuals serve as evidence—assuming that the motivation for such attacks lies solely in the victims' poverty—there is often a failure, whether conscious or not, to examine the passports of those affected. Likewise, little attention is paid to the social stereotype embodied by people in street situations in Spain.

The answers to these two questions may prove revealing: More often than not, these individuals are immigrants—or, socially, they embody the stereotype of the undocumented immigrant, pejoratively labeled "illegal," perceived as a threat to social peace through their mere presence and ultimately associated with criminality. This image is particularly prevalent in relation to non-European immigrants, especially those from Latin American countries.

Another element that stands out is the effort to establish—at all costs—a connection between criminal law and aporophobia by using crimes committed against homeless individuals in that country, while at the same time acknowledging the absence of empirical or statistical data to substantiate such an endeavor. Instead, the phenomenon is attributed to the so-called hidden figure.[11]

What is even more striking, however, is the lack of any link between this phenomenon and the fact that undocumented immigrants are unable to resort to criminal law to protect their legal interests—assuming, of course, that criminal law protects anything at all—yet they are still subjected to the full force of its selective application.

From a methodological standpoint, we might say that the field itself is pointing the way forward; any deviation from this path seems not only forced but also the result of a certain investigative myopia, which can lead to completely unpredictable outcomes. In other words, even in that country, it becomes clear that analysis must be local. That said, we will not delve into the specific Spanish case here, although we believe that—with the necessary adjustments—this analysis could very well apply to that reality.

This epistemological error becomes even more evident when one considers the hasty attempt to explain the profound selectivity of punitive power in Brazil through the notion of aporophobia. Whether due to the reasons previously discussed or simply because—given the scale of our uncontrolled exercise of punitive power—it would be more accurate to speak, in fact, of a kind of Brazilianophobia.

2.2 Aporophobia: A Failed Critical-Criminological Concept

Aporophobia can be described as a failed critical-criminological concept. Despite the efforts made—particularly from penal idealism—to frame it as a suitable tool for criticizing the exercise of punitive power, it ultimately produces diffuse, abstract, and empirically inconsistent notions, especially when addressing punitive power as a recognized, hypercomplex phenomenon.

What is missing here is radicality as a central heuristic element—something aporophobia cannot offer precisely because its very definition is generalist. In the criminological-critical field, at least in its modern formulation, any criminological analysis that aims to be truly critical must be *radical.*

This radicality is not connected—at least not directly—to the old radical criminology of Marxist origin (or rather, Marxian),[12] but instead refers to the indispensable depth, precision, and atomic detailing required in any analysis that precedes meaningful critique.

In short, when we speak of radicality, we are referring to the criminological capacity to uncover the most deeply submerged roots of the issue under examination—the very opposite of what the notion of aporophobia, as a supposed criminological concept, promotes.

This is because its approach attempts to encompass an endless array of heuristic elements that constitute the exercise of punitive power, flattening the entire *ethnoscape* and reducing the complexity of the phenomenon to a notion of poverty rooted in the previous century. This move, in addition to being methodologically inadequate, is criminologically unorthodox.

Aporophobia, through its generic insistence on poverty and its consequent economic reductionism, clings to a framework of power that no longer exists: one shaped by the old welfare state—or approximations of it[13]—anchored in productive capitalism, where social dynamics were characterized by a dialectical logic dominated by the binary relationship between *exploiter and exploited.*[14]

Within that power framework, the exercise of punitive power—that is, formal social control—was directed at those who either refused or, for various reasons, were unable to consume, in addition to serving its traditional function of keeping the exploited, controlled, and, above all, domesticated.[15]

The current framework of power corresponds to that of financial capitalism, which subordinates the productive sphere, undermines the achievements of the welfare state and its consumer society, and is driven by a new dynamic of inclusion and exclusion. Within this logic, the so-called *30/70 society prevails*[16]: Thirty percent included, seventy percent excluded. In this model, the included no longer need the excluded; it is, therefore, a non-dialectical model.[17]

From this new form of segregation—established as a mark of global power—emerges the evidence that power, in its multiple dimensions, now directs itself toward controlling the excluded. These are no longer seen as conjunctural, transitory, or circumstantial, but rather as structural and structuring.[18] In practical terms, this model helps explain the contemporary reproduction of violence, especially in our region.

A defining feature of the theoretical attempt to link aporophobia to the old configuration of power—no longer existent in the current historical moment—is the belief that the ideological foundation of uncontrolled punitive power lies in this or that penal theory. Such an approach allows the current mark of power to slip by unnoticed, despite being the true engine behind today's punitive disorder. Moreover, it reduces the ideological foundations to those forged strictly within the penal field, reproducing a linearity that is incompatible with the necessary interdisciplinarity inherent in the ideological construction of complex phenomena such as power—especially punitive power.

Furthermore, when the so-called ideological bases of aporophobic criminal law are identified with the theoretical currents of *radical functionalism, managerialism, actuarialism, and punitivism*, what we see is nothing more than a rebranded application of critical postulates developed in the last century, designed to address a very different configuration of global power.

These theoretical frameworks no longer correspond to the premises under which they were formed. The enemies they once named are not the same—formerly the foreigner or the supposed "terrorist." The cost-benefit logic to which they once referred has given way to a new relationship of functionality tied to today's dominant power dynamics. Criminal law, in this context, expands not merely through penal punitivism but is pluralized into a multitude of forms through which punitive power is exercised.[19]

Thus, this theoretical movement fails to present an authentic *critique of ideology*, as it practically ignores the current configuration of power and its falsely liberal legitimizing ideology.[20] At best, it offers a critique of isolated theories, as if a single theoretical strand could be *primarily responsible* for sustaining an entire system—rather than the system itself shaping those theories.[21]

This lack of critique directed at the overarching ideology that sustains the current disorder of punitive power stems from an unwillingness—or inability—to challenge the reductionism inherent in any such legitimizing ideology. To do so would require exposing how simplification and distance from reality function as mechanisms of concealment. In other words, a critique of ideology must rest on revealing what brings us closer to—or separates us from—reality itself.[22]

If the idea of aporophobia, when presented as a criminological concept, is itself a reductionist and simplistic representation of the complexity of punitive power, then how could it possibly serve as a tool to critique ideologies constructed through the very same mechanisms?

2.3 Epistemological Bases of Aporophobia as a Critical Criminological Concept

To approach the critique of punitive power through aporophobia as a critical criminological concept—that is, to frame its selectivity using this generic matrix, supposedly compatible with any time and historical context—represents a regression to the errors of early criminological critique. It also disregards an undeniable aspect of reality: The selectivity of punitive power, which such early critique once addressed, no longer presents itself in the same terms, given the shift in the current configuration of power.[23] our margins, *this selectivity has become, in fact, abysmal.*[24]

This theoretical movement is, in truth, a return to the criminological critique of Marxist origin, which—despite its valuable contributions to penal discourse[25]—manifested as a partial critique, practicing a kind of economic determinism that portrayed the offender either as a passive subject detached from class responsibility or as a revolutionary hero acting on behalf of that very class.[26] There is no need to revisit the well-known epistemological misconceptions of this critical tradition within criminology.

The other face of this monolithic view of punitive power—which treats aporophobia as a kind of return to the past—is that of the early pioneers of critical thought who, working from a positivist framework, undertook the first efforts to translate the postulates of historical materialism into criminology.

These studies were fundamentally important for the development of critical thought, despite their positivist orientation—something entirely understandable given their historical context. It would be anachronistic to evaluate their theoretical contributions by today's standards.[27] However, to promote a return to such determinism in our present context, marked by the increasing complexity of the phenomena surrounding punitive power, would be unthinkable.

The notion of an aporophobic criminal law is, in fact, grounded ideologically—within the penal field—in the belief that the expansion of the welfare state is responsible for the reduction of crime rates. In other words, once the so-called social causes of crime were addressed, crime would decrease to nearly zero.[28]

This stance, based on an idealistic view of punitive power, ends up attributing crime, to some extent, to individual causes. An important movement in this direction was initiated by the German alternative project which, despite its political-criminal advances toward a minimal and reparative criminal law,[29] creates an idealistic determinism regarding criminal law and social dynamics themselves.

This seems to be one of the main theoretical matrices that influence the idea of an aporophobic criminal law, hastily elevating aporophobia to the status of a critical criminological concept. Ideologically, it could be said that the true foundation of the emergence of this supposedly critical perspective—a partial critique, it would be more accurate to say—is the traditional juridical-penal idealism, shaped by a criminal policy that claims to be empirical while operating deductively. Added to this is a critical posture that is, to a large extent, uninformed both criminologically and, above all, sociologically.

Evidence of this can be found in the attempt to transpose a positivist perspective—albeit a critical one—onto a welfare state ideal that, at least in Brazil, we have never experienced. In our Latin American margins, this ideal has taken the form of intermittent experimentation with substantive citizenship, promoted occasionally by progressive governments.

2.4 Theoretical Migrations and Their Epistemological Dangers

Theories are not aseptic at any global latitude. They are shaped, to a large extent, by the intricate relationship between the interpretation of the specific world for which they were conceived and the ideology of those who conceived them.

Understanding this dynamic sets the tone for the epistemological complexity involved in applying a given theory or concept to different realities—not because of their undeniable political character, which ideologically circumscribes them (something widely accepted in modern thought, even seen as a marker of intellectual honesty), but above all because of the need for theoretical-methodological adaptation inherent to all theoretical importation—if not outright rejection due to insurmountable inadequacy.

Theoretical concepts are not importable products universally compatible with all historical and social contexts. Even material goods must pass through customs checks before crossing borders—meaning that, in the world of tangible things, some degree of qualitative verification is required to ensure compliance with the standards of their intended destination.

Obviously, this comparison is only metaphorical, meant to illustrate the imperative of scrutinizing what comes from outside. Even in a globalized and interconnected world,[30] imported ideas are formed by different standards. In the theoretical field, this calls for a qualitative criterion rooted in the principle of *adequacy*.

The uncritical importation of theories and concepts—without prior assessment of their relevance—almost always leads to genuine theoretical disasters, with highly tangible consequences in the world of life. When this occurs in the penal or criminological field, the consequences are even more serious: The issue is not just one of methodological adequacy or inadequacy, but of an epistemological-methodological misunderstanding that ultimately ends up directly or indirectly legitimizing the current penal reality.

This legitimization—particularly in Brazil, where punitive power is uncontrolled and abysmally selective—operates through the normalization of this state of affairs, which comes to be seen as natural under the illusion that all theoretical efforts to find practical solutions have already been fairly and adequately pursued.

This normalizing logic is also responsible for acting as a barrier to any truly emancipatory theoretical-critical production guided by a *decolonial* lens and rooted in empirical realities that shape the current criminal landscape. In doing so, it actively resists and denies all forms of automatic theoretical importation, a phenomenon we might call *theoretical foreignism.*

2.5 Theoretical Late-Colonialism

Obviously, we are not a theoretical island detached from global knowledge production—quite the contrary. We must foster bridges, connections, interconnections, and theoretical crossroads, since complex problems demand integrative, interdisciplinary, and epistemologically grounded responses.[31]

Nor do we advocate for the rejection of all knowledge produced elsewhere, ignoring the fact that science knows no borders and that many centers of excellence undeniably lie beyond our own. We cannot disregard the methodological rigor of German criminal law dogmatics, the transformative potential of Italian criminological critique, the creative energy of Spanish criminal policy, and a long list of other contributions.

This is not a call for denial, but rather for the recognition that these theoretical perspectives were forged within particular realities, and that their application cannot be universal or automatic. In the social sciences—and law is a social science, let that be clear—the empirical world is not a given. It must be apprehended and interpreted in ways that are historically and contextually grounded, which is only possible through theoretical instruments that incorporate, as a central element, the reality that surrounds them.

In this sense, when it comes to theories and concepts produced abroad, our approach should be to critically incorporate what is useful, discard what is not, and critique what operates in reverse. This requires cultivating a questioning attitude—one especially necessary given our condition as late-colonized societies in the broadest sense—so that this condition does not continue to reproduce itself in the theoretical field, thereby legitimizing, in one way or another, our subordinate position.

To treat theoretical foreignism as inherently positive, or to adopt imported theories automatically, is to accept—even if unconsciously—the idea that we are passive consumers of what is produced across the sea. Instead, we must embrace the notion that we are capable of creating new knowledge from our own reality—not out of a mere desire for innovation, but in response to the pressing need to address the specific problems we face.

In this way, generalist and diffuse critical perspectives—which do little to transform the underlying dynamics of punitive selectivity—become not only functional to the system, but also a strategic mechanism for sustaining the ideology that underpins the exclusionary logic of financial capitalism and its false narratives that obscure sociopolitical reality.

2.6 Theories That Chirp Here Do Not Chirp There

The practical repercussions of theoretical concepts vary fundamentally depending on the time and space in which they are applied. This, in itself, already affirms that every theoretical concept corresponds to a specific reality. While it gives practical substance to the aphorism that "there is nothing as practical as a good theory,"[32] it is equally true that a bad—or inadequate—theory (which amounts to the same) also produces concrete and well-defined practical consequences.

In this sense, the idea of *criminal law of the enemy*, initially popularized in Germany—though its epistemological roots are much older, Germany being merely the place of its explicit naming[33]—generates, in that social reality, a movement of exacerbation of punitive power. This results in disastrous outcomes, particularly for rightless subjects, such as stereotyped and undocumented immigrants.

In other words, we might say that the practical result of this "exceptional criminal law" is a more or less controlled increase in imprisonment rates for these vulnerable groups, combined with heightened intolerance—or zero tolerance—toward them.

Ultimately, the result of this theoretical stance in that country does not go far beyond the imprisonment of a few more immigrants or vulnerable individuals. This is undoubtedly deplorable; however, it is not possible to deny that its impact is still relatively controlled—at least if we analyze it through the lens of comparative criminal policy.

In Brazil, and more broadly in Latin America, we produce our own enemies. Those who suffer under the intensified selectivity of punitive power do not carry, in our peculiar reality, different passports. They are Brazilian—indeed, they are historically responsible for the very idea of Brazil in the world of life: Black and Brown people, heirs to a slaveholding legacy that neither our state nor our society has ever overcome.

The abysmal selectivity of punitive power in Brazil affects not only a specific, extremely broad segment of marginalized citizens but does so with an intensity unseen in other latitudes. This is evident in the high levels of police lethality, mass incarceration, and the vicious cycle generated by the exclusionary logic on which this selectivity is based.

Another field that illustrates how theories do not echo in our Brazilian (or Latin American) margin as they do in other hemispheres is that of the classic punishment-justifying theories (the world of *ought to be*). Their various classifications—general and special preventions—are already questionable from a realist standpoint, given the lack of empirical evidence supporting their effectiveness. On the contrary, recent criminological research exposes the fallacy of these categorizations (the *world of ought to be*).[34]

This contrast becomes even more striking when we observe the reality of Brazilian punitive power in relation to these supposed theoretical categorizations. To think of the resocializing function of punishment already requires a suspension of disbelief,[35] but to do so in Brazil amounts to a collective theoretical delusion—one that only serves to legitimize the excessive action of punitive power, granting it a noble function. And yet, it is equally questionable, for it is not the role of the state to assume the practically theological mission of *saving souls* through resocialization.

What we must illuminate, among other things, is the capacity of certain strains of theoretical idealism to legitimize punitive power in our region—particularly in

Brazil, where punitive selectivity reaches abysmal depths. Placing everything in its proper context, and understanding that theories resonate differently within our social reality due to the sheer intensity of punitive violence, is essential to the initial overcoming of this abysmal selectivity.

The attempt to elevate aporophobia to the status of a critical-criminological concept is, in many ways, a wager on that same idealism. More than that, it appears to be its very product: It feeds on the notion that poverty is the root of all punitive selectivity, as if reducing poverty would automatically reduce crime—much like the proponents of the German alternative draft once believed. This view neglects the reality of economic crime and falls back into the old deterministic framework of critical criminology, which disregards the systemic functionality of subsistence-based offenses within the current power structure.

2.7 The Brazilian Slaveholding Heritage and Punitive Power

Every society has a historical matrix that sustains the selectivity of its local punitive power. In Brazil, there is no doubt that this matrix is slavery: foundational to Brazilian society and, after its formal abolition, continued through abandonment and criminalization—especially via property-related offenses—and through lethal violence that continues to shape the social imaginary to this day.

All Brazilian political, legal, and social institutions structurally incorporate and reproduce this racist scar—not as something occasional or intermittent, but with a permanence and intensity rarely seen elsewhere with such refinement. As a consequence, it can be said that in Brazil, "the viability of the systemic reproduction of racist practices is embedded in the political, economic, and legal organization of society. Racism is expressed concretely as political, economic, and legal inequality."[36]

This historical element, which fuels the selectivity of punitive power in Brazil, has long been rendered invisible by the social sciences as a whole through the narrative of *racial democracy*. This narrative masks the deep-rooted negative conception of Brazil's ethnodiversity beneath an alleged celebration of the "three races" that supposedly constitute the national identity. Academic discourse played an essential role in cementing the mythical harmony between the *big house* and the *slave quarters*.[37]

It is impossible to understand punitive power in Brazil without first addressing structural racism—its historical origins, its direct consequences in the prison system, and, from there, its intersection with other sociopolitical markers.

Data from the penal system allow us to both see and reveal—also through quantitative means—the enduring influence of the country's slaveholding legacy on the operation of punitive power. Brazil has one of the largest prison populations in the world, with more than 852,000 incarcerated individuals—a staggering representation of how this selective system is deeply racialized.[38]

When we examine the latest statistics on the socioeconomic composition of Brazil's prison population, we find a powerful quantitative confirmation of our prior critique. Without this data, the argument could too easily be dismissed as merely speculative. The numbers show that 69.1% of Brazil's prison population is composed of Black or Brown people.[39] That means nearly two-thirds of those incarcerated are from historically marginalized and racialized social groups—heirs to the legacy of slavery.

In a complementary and tragic movement—marked by a criminal policy of "tears and blood"—the extremely high levels of state lethality further confirm this perverse preference for Black and Brown bodies, especially young ones, effectively constituting a kind of genocide. No longer a *drip*, as Latin American criminological critique once warned in the previous century, the floodgates of violence against the vulnerable have now been fully opened.[40]

Statistics from 2021 show that 77.1% of homicide victims in Brazil were Black or Brown.[41] When disaggregated by population, this means that 31 out of every 100,000 Black or Brown Brazilians were murdered, compared to only 10.8 among non-Black or Brown individuals.[42] Both figures are abhorrent—this must be emphasized—but there is no doubt about the racial dimension of Brazil's unchecked punitive lethality.

These data become even more alarming when we consider their impact on young people. Among Black and Brown males aged 15–29, the homicide rate reaches 94.4 and 136.5 per 100,000, respectively.[43] In the same demographic group among white individuals, this rate drops to 41.6. These are the figures of a war—one that generates profound and ongoing social destabilization.[44]

This convergence of mass incarceration and lethal violence—targeting a specific social subject—cannot be dismissed as a coincidence. Any researcher grounded in material reality would heuristically perceive this thread that runs through Brazil's punitive power. And this should not be confused with the notion that poverty alone explains the intensification of punitive selectivity.

Yes, those represented in these statistics are poor—but in Brazil, poverty feeds on racism. They are not Black or Brown *because* they are poor; they are poor *because* they are Black or Brown. To overlook this intersection, that is, to disregard the racialization of poverty in Brazil, is to erase the central factor that drives punitive selectivity in Brazil.

When aporophobia is framed as a critical criminological concept, it dissolves into air under a wholly economicist interpretation of reality. It attributes the exponential rise in penal selectivity primarily to economic aversion—hatred of the poor and of poverty—thus derailing any truly transformative critique.

Brazil's own economic dynamics refute this logic. It echoes old Keynesian notions, translated into penal terms by the German alternative draft, in which greater socioeconomic development was expected to produce lower crime rates. However, this theory has not been empirically validated in Europe—and certainly not in our Southern margins, where we have experienced only brief expansions of substantive citizenship, usually under progressive governments, and never a welfare state in any real sense.

Between 2000 and 2013, Brazil had one of the fastest-growing economies in the world.[45] This growth was accompanied by concrete gains in citizenship, income distribution, access to rights, and quality of life for the working class. Millions were lifted out of poverty.

Yet, this economically vibrant context did *not* result in reduced incarceration or diminished state lethality. On the contrary, the graph tracking economic growth until 2013 was mirrored by the growth in penal selectivity—both displaying the same racial profile.

This alone should suffice to show that the selectivity of punitive power—whether in Brazil or elsewhere—is multifaceted. It cannot be reduced to economic factors alone, nor, consequently, to the idea of aporophobia.

Any emancipatory critique must be able to identify the main *microsocial matrix* that sustains punitive power at a given historical time and in a given place. To retreat into a criminological critique based on poverty—or a phobia of the poor, which is practically the same—is to romanticize and fetishize poverty under reversed terms. It traps us within the eternal dichotomy of oppressed and oppressor, while failing to see the deeply rooted and layered nature of this relationship. In Brazil, that foundational layer is the *slaveholding scar*.

Notes

1. Zaffaroni, R. & Dias Dos Santos, Í. (2019). *La nueva crítica criminológica: Criminología en tiempos de totalitarismo financiero*. Buenos Aires: Ediar.
2. Souza, J. (2017). *A elite do atraso: da escravidão à Lava Jato*. Rio de Janeiro: Leya, pp. 36 ff.
3. Souza, J. (2020). *A guerra contra o Brasil*. Rio de Janeiro: Estação Brasil, pp. 22 ff.
4. Santos, M. (2001). *Por uma outra globalização*. Rio de Janeiro: Record, pp. 37 ff.; Beck, U. (2008). *¿Qué es la globalización? Falacias del globalismo, respuestas a la globalización*. Barcelona: Paidós, pp. 31 ff.
5. Chapman, D. (1971). *Lo stereotipo del criminale*. Torino: Einaudi; Mazzara, B. M. (1997). *Stereotipi e pregiudizi*. Bologna: Il Mulino.
6. Borges, J. (2019). *Encarceramento em massa*. São Paulo: Pólen Produção Editorial LTDA, p. 41.
7. Moreira, A. (2019). *Racismo recreativo*. São Paulo: Pólen, pp. 66 ff.
8. Sousa Santos, B. (2018). *Esquerdas do mundo, uni-vos*. São Paulo: Boitempo.
9. Bustos Rubio, M. (2020). *Aporofobia y delito: La discriminación socioeconómica como agravante (art. 22, 4ª CP)*. Barcelona: JM Bosch.
10. The same could be said of other criminological contexts, such as that of the United States, where the hermeneutic key to understanding the selectivity of punitive power appears to be structural racism against African Americans, combined with xenophobia directed at immigrants of Latin American origin. See: Alexander, M. (2012). *The New Jim Crow: Mass Incarceration in the Age of Colorblindness*. New York: The New Press.
11. García Domínguez, I. (2020). *La aporofobia en el sistema penal español: Especial referencia al colectivo de personas sin hogar*. Salamanca: Ratio Legis.
12. On the origins of this criminology, see: Greenberg, D. F. (Ed.). *Crime and Capitalism: Readings in Marxist Criminology*. Palo Alto: Mayfield Publishing Company, 1981, pp. 38

ff.; also, Rusche, G. & Kirchheimer, O. *Pena y estructura social*. Bogotá: Temis, 1984, pp. 16 ff.

13. In our region, we have never experienced a welfare state in the terms seen in Northern Hemisphere countries. What prevailed here was a certain expansion of substantive citizenship promoted by progressive governments. See: Zaffaroni, R. & Dias Dos Santos, Í. (2020). *La nueva crítica criminológica: Criminología en tiempos de totalitarismo financiero*. Valencia: Tirant lo Blanch, pp. 27 ff.
14. Martin, H.-P. & Schumann, H. (1996). *Die Globalisierungsfalle: Der Angriff auf Demokratie und Wohlstand*. Hamburg: Rowohlt Verlag, pp. 7 ff.
15. Zaffaroni, R. & Dias Dos Santos, Í. (2020). *La nueva crítica criminológica: Criminología en tiempos de totalitarismo financiero*. Valencia: Tirant lo Blanch, pp. 27 ff.
16. Martin, H.-P. & Schumann, H. (1996). *Die Globalisierungsfalle: Der Angriff auf Demokratie und Wohlstand*. Hamburg: Rowohlt Verlag, pp. 7 ff.
17. Zaffaroni, R. & Dias Dos Santos, Í. (2020). *La nueva crítica criminológica: Criminología en tiempos de totalitarismo financiero*. Valencia: Tirant lo Blanch, pp. 27 ff.
18. On power and its phenomenological dimensions, see: Foucault, M. (2013). *La société punitive: Cours au Collège de France (1972–1973)*. Paris: EHESS Gallimard Seuil, pp. 231 ff.
19. Lodoño Berrío, H. L. (2016). *Sistemas punitivos y derechos humanos: El caso de la Comuna 13 de Medellín—Colombia*. Bogotá: Ediciones Jurídicas Andrés Morales, pp. xxiii ff.
20. Zaffaroni, R. & Dias Dos Santos, Í. (2020). *La nueva crítica criminológica: Criminología en tiempos de totalitarismo financiero*. Op. cit., pp. 55 ff.
21. In fact, it is the system that feeds the theories, which in turn attempt to legitimize it—either directly or indirectly.
22. Zaffaroni, R. & Dias Dos Santos, Í. (2020). *La nueva crítica criminológica: Criminología en tiempos de totalitarismo financiero*. Op. cit., pp. 55 ff.
23. Zaffaroni, R. & Dias Dos Santos, Í. (2020). *La nueva crítica criminológica: Criminología en tiempos de totalitarismo financiero*. Op. cit., pp. 55 ff.
24. Dias dos Santos, Í. (2021). *La perenne expansión del poder punitivo: Una selectividad jurídico-penal abisal*. Buenos Aires: BdeF.
25. Melossi, D. & Pavarini, M. (2018). *Carcere e fabbrica: Alle origini del sistema penitenziario*. Bologna: Società Editrice il Mulino, pp. 15 ff.
26. Larrauri, E. (2000). *La herencia de la criminología crítica*. Madrid: Siglo Veintiuno de España, pp. 25 ff.
27. One should not conduct historiographic analysis using the parameters of a different historical period.
28. On this point, see a valuable analysis of the well-known alternative draft to the German Penal Code in: Roxin, C. (1976). *Problemas básicos del derecho penal*. Madrid: Reus, pp. 42 ff.
29. Dias dos Santos, Í. (2018). *En busca de la justicia restaurativa: Un cambio de paradigma en el derecho penal de garantías*. Buenos Aires/Montevideo: BdeF.
30. Castells, M. (1998). *La era de la información: Economía, sociedad y cultura. Volumen I. La sociedad red*. Madrid: Alianza Editorial, p. 28.
31. Sousa Santos, B. (2017). *Justicia entre saberes: Epistemologías del Sur contra el epistemicidio*. Madrid: Akal, pp. 289 ff.
32. Lewin, K. (1988). *La teoría del campo en la ciencia social*. Buenos Aires/Barcelona: Ediciones Paidós, p. 161.
33. Zaffaroni, R. (2006). *El enemigo en el derecho penal*. Madrid: Dykinson.
34. Zaffaroni, R. (1993). *Hacia un realismo jurídico penal marginal*. Caracas: Monte Ávila Editores Latinoamericana, pp. 9 ff.
35. Muñoz Conde, F. (1979). *La resocialización del delincuente: Análisis y crítica de un mito*. In: *Sistema: Revista de Ciencias Sociales*, n. 31, pp. 73–84. In the same vein, see:

Bettiol, G. (1963). *Il mito della rieducazione*. In: *Rivista Italiana di Diritto e Procedura Penale*, n. 3, v. 6, pp. 701 ff.

36. Almeida, S. (2019). *Racismo estrutural*. São Paulo: Pólen Editorial, p. 33.
37. On the myth of racial democracy in Brazil, see: Oliveira Pires, T. R. (2018). *Estruturas intocadas: Racismo e ditadura no Rio de Janeiro*. In: *Revista Direito e Práxis*, v. 9, n. 2, pp. 1056 ff. In the same critical sense, see also: Borges, J. (2020). *Prisões: Espelhos de nós*. São Paulo: Todavia, pp. 14 ff.
38. Fórum Brasileiro de Segurança Pública. (2024). *Anuário Brasileiro de Segurança Pública*. São Paulo: FBSP.
39. Fórum Brasileiro de Segurança Pública. (2024). *Anuário Brasileiro de Segurança Pública*. São Paulo: FBSP, p. 360.
40. In the same sense, see the work of Oliveira Pires, T. R. (2017). *Criminologia crítica e pacto narcísico: Por uma crítica criminológica apreensível em pretuguês*. In: *Revista Brasileira de Ciências Criminais*, v. 135, ano 25, p. 557—especially where she teaches us that "genocide, as a practice imposed on Black people in Brazil, offers a concrete explanatory key for the operational model of racism over our bodies." For a broader analysis, see also the classic work of Nascimento, A. (1978). *O genocídio do negro brasileiro: Processo de um racismo mascarado*. Rio de Janeiro: Paz e Terra, pp. 41 ff.
41. This is the most recent data point in the historical series released by the Brazilian public authorities.
42. Instituto de Pesquisa Econômica Aplicada; Fórum Brasileiro de Segurança Pública. (2023). *Atlas da Violência 2023*. Brasília/Rio de Janeiro/São Paulo: IPEA, pp. 53 ff.
43. Instituto Brasileiro de Geografia e Estatística. (2022). *Desigualdades sociais por cor ou raça no Brasil. Estudos e Pesquisas—Informações demográficas e econômicas*, 2ª ed., n. 48. Rio de Janeiro: IBGE, pp. 1–16.
44. Instituto Brasileiro de Geografia e Estatística. (2022). *Desigualdades sociais por cor ou raça no Brasil. Estudos e Pesquisas—Informações demográficas e econômicas*, 2ª ed., n. 48. Rio de Janeiro: IBGE, pp. 1–16.
45. Data from the International Monetary Fund (IMF), *World Economic Outlook (WEO) Report*.

Bibliography

Alexander, M. (2012). *The new Jim Crow: Mass incarceration in the age of colorblindness*. The New Press.

Almeida, S. (2019). *Racismo estrutural*. Pólen Editorial.

Beck, U. (2008). *¿qué es la globalización? Falacias del globalismo, respuestas a la globalización*. Paidós.

Bettiol, G. (1963). Il mito della rieducazione. *Rivista Italiana di Diritto e Procedura Penale, 3*(6).

Borges, J. (2019). *Encarceramento em massa*. Pólen Produção Editorial LTDA.

Borges, J. (2020). *Prisões: Espelhos de nós*. Todavia.

Bustos Rubio, M. (2020). *Aporofobia y delito: La discriminación socioeconómica como agravante (art. 22, 4ª CP)*. JM Bosch.

Castells, M. (1998). *La era de la información: Economía, sociedad y cultura. Volumen i. la sociedad red*. Alianza Editorial.

Chapman, D. (1971). *Lo Stereotipo del criminale*. Einaudi.

Dias Dos Santos, Í. (2018). *En busca de la justicia restaurativa: Un cambio de paradigma en el derecho penal de garantías*. BdeF.

Dias Dos Santos, Í. (2021). *La perenne expansión del poder punitivo: Una selectividad jurídico-penal abisal*. BdeF.

Fórum Brasileiro de Segurança Pública. (2024). *Anuário Brasileiro de Segurança Pública*. FBSP.
Foucault, M. (2013). *La société punitive: Cours au Collège de France (1972–1973)*. EHESS Gallimard Seuil.
García Domínguez, I. (2020). *La aporofobia en el sistema penal español: Especial referencia al colectivo de personas sin hogar*. Ratio Legis.
Greenberg, D. F. (Ed.). (1981). *Crime and capitalism: Readings in Marxist criminology*. Mayfield Publishing Company.
Instituto Brasileiro de Geografia e Estatística. (2022). Desigualdades sociais por cor ou raça no Brasil. *Estudos e Pesquisas – Informações demográficas e econômicas*, 2ª ed., 48. IBGE.
Instituto de Pesquisa Econômica Aplicada; Fórum Brasileiro de Segurança Pública. (2023). *Atlas da Violência 2023*. IPEA.
International Monetary Fund (IMF). *World Economic Outlook (WEO) Report*.
Larrauri, E. (2000). *La herencia de la criminología crítica*. Siglo Veintiuno de España.
Lewin, K. (1988). *La teoría del campo en la ciencia social*. Ediciones Paidós.
Lodoño Berrío, H. L. (2016). *Sistemas punitivos y derechos humanos: El caso de la Comuna 13 de medellín – Colombia*. Ediciones Jurídicas Andrés Morales.
Martin, H.-P., & Schumann, H. (1996). *Die Globalisierungsfalle: Der Angriff auf Demokratie und Wohlstand*. Rowohlt Verlag.
Mazzara, B. M. (1997). *Stereotipi e pregiudizi*. Il Mulino.
Melossi, D., & Pavarini, M. (2018). *Carcere e fabbrica: Alle origini del sistema penitenziario*. Società Editrice il Mulino.
Moreira, A. (2019). *Racismo recreativo*. Pólen.
Muños Conde, F. (1979). La resocialización del delincuente: Análisis y crítica de un mito. *Sistema: Revista de Ciencias Sociales*, 31.
Nascimento, A. (1978). *O genocídio do negro brasileiro: Processo de um racismo mascarado*. Paz e Terra.
Pires, T. R. (2017). Criminologia crítica e pacto narcísico: Por uma crítica criminológica apreensível em pretuguês. *Revista Brasileira de Ciências Criminais*, *ano25*(135),
Pires, T. R. (2018). Estruturas intocadas: Racismo e ditadura no Rio de Janeiro. *Revista Direito e Práxis*, *9*(2).
Rusche, G., & Kirchheimer, O. (1984). *Pena y estructura social*. Temis.
Sousa Santos, B. (2017). *Justicia entre saberes: Epistemologías del sur contra el epistemicidio*. Akal.
Sousa Santos, B. (2018). *Esquerdas do mundo, uni-vos*. Boitempo.
Souza, J. (2017). *A elite do atraso: da escravidão à Lava Jato*. Leya.
Souza, J. (2020). *A guerra contra o Brasil*. Estação Brasil.
Zaffaroni, R. (1993). *Hacia un realismo jurídico penal marginal*. Monte Ávila Editores Latinoamericana.
Zaffaroni, R. (2006). *El enemigo en el derecho penal*. Dykinson.
Zaffaroni, R., & Dias Dos Santos, Í. (2019). *La nueva crítica criminológica: Criminología En Tiempos de Totalitarismo Financiero*. Ediar.
Zaffaroni, R., & Dias Dos Santos, Í. (2020). *La nueva crítica criminológica: Criminología En Tiempos de Totalitarismo Financiero*. Tirant lo Blanch.

Chapter 3
The Criminal Policy of the "Other"

3.1 Different Levels of Citizens

To *see* and *make* visible the *current criminal policy of the other*—marked by mass incarceration and high lethality toward historically vulnerable groups, and practiced in Brazil as a state policy, that is, one undertaken by governments of the most diverse political-ideological stripes—it is essential to approach the very idea of the Rule of Law.

Not only because a truly democratic criminal policy can only emerge from a healthy Rule of Law, but also because any criminal policy that deviates from it contains the dangerous germ capable of gradually transmuting that ideal into something altogether different from the constitutional promise of democracy, thus eroding the very conditions of the state's existence.[1] It is precisely along this path—and at giant steps—that the Brazilian case advances.

From a realistic and critical perspective, this analysis must begin with an almost archeological gaze: one capable of uncovering the residual fragments of a state model that has all but disintegrated, shaping something entirely distant from the model once envisioned.

Some elements of that former model persist merely as civilizational memory; they are no longer part of lived reality. The current Brazilian state model not only deviates from the promised Rule of Law but appears to choose, deliberately, the opposite direction—and the criminal question functions as one of the primary catalysts of this drift.

In this context, the media invention—nonexistent, yet with very real effects—of a caste of *pariahs*, built upon racist stereotypes and imagined as an agglomeration of inferior human beings (*Untermenschen*), destined to be subjected to all forms of unlimited punishment and even extermination, operates as an endogenous force that dismantles the Rule of Law through the uncontrolled exercise of punitive power.

Í. Dias Dos Santos, *Aporophobia and Punitive Power in Brazil*,
SpringerBriefs in Criminology,
https://doi.org/10.1007/978-3-032-01753-6_3

This lack of control intensifies as the image of this supposed caste of *pariahs* is arbitrarily projected onto a broad category of historically vulnerable people in the country. This enables local executive agencies to carry out an almost unlimited criminalizing selection—a selection guided not by legality, but by prejudice, at the moment of distinguishing between "thieves" and "non-thieves."

Such uncontrolled exercise of punitive power constitutes a central mechanism of a genuine state policy which, through action or omission, increasingly consolidates a kind of *caste state*, structured upon the aberrant notion that there exist different "levels of citizens"—a notion that shapes the legal, social, and political dynamics of the country.

The criminal policy that defines this *caste state* is what we call the criminal policy of the other: one that directs its repressive gaze toward an "other" with whom no one wishes to identify, and toward whom no empathy is extended—a *Nicht-Person* (nonperson), held biologically responsible for all the country's criminality in a near-biological movement of blame.

3.2 The Rule of Law: The Unkept Promise

The set of constitutional norms configures a sort of imperative promise—a reaffirmation of what is meant to be, ought to be, and is desired as a state. From this perspective, constitutional norms in a broad sense—whether rules or principles—have the nature of imperative mandates, allowing no margin for their implementation to be postponed indefinitely. In other words, they are constant demands of the *here and now*.[2]

Although the realization of these norms in social reality obviously requires an action plan that can only unfold gradually over time, the constitutional norm cannot serve as a pretext for an endless deferral of implementation.[3] Therefore, its assessment must be carried out through careful observation of the direction in which that plan is oriented.[4]

Put differently, if observation reveals that the implementation plan moves in a completely different direction, it must be concluded that the issue is not merely a natural delay in the path to realization, but rather the disregard of the constitutional mandate—a failure to fulfill the promise enshrined in the Constitution.

Setting aside the well-worn distinction between formal and substantive equality—the former being meaningless without the latter[5]—the truth is that the principle of equality is one of the core values of the Rule of Law and of democracy itself, for it gives content to both by enabling the real conditions for democratic coexistence.[6] Without promoting actual equality among its citizens, the Rule of Law becomes inconceivable.

In Brazil, the actual social implementation of the constitutional promise of a Rule of Law seems to proceed in the opposite direction of the supreme normative mandate. This march of reality against the normative ought is evidenced, above all, in the growing and alarming inequality that—rather than diminishing—intensifies in Brazilian society (among the most unequal on the planet).[7] As in much of the peripheral world, our Rule of Law becomes increasingly formal, while constitutionalism deteriorates into mere symbolism.[8]

This breach of the constitutional promise leads, in practice, to the configuration of an immunodepressed state—an institutional framework incapable of guaranteeing the minimum conditions for peaceful coexistence and even less for the realization of its citizens, since no society can achieve such coexistence when structured around impermeable castes that freeze social mobility, allowing a few to live decently while the many are denied even the basic means of survival.

The movement away from the legal ought of the constitution not only opens space but actively promotes—through action or omission—a real internal war of survival governed by the law of the strongest, generating among the most socially vulnerable a vicious cycle of accelerated production and reproduction of marginalization.[9]

This divergence between the constitutional mandate and lived reality results in the state's reduced capacity to protect its citizens. It fails to implement policies that mitigate inequality and foster social and human development—policies that would be essential for realizing the principle of equality.

As a result of this omission, the number of vulnerable individuals grows rapidly—and so too does the need to control them. It is, therefore, the repressive face of the state that gains increasing protagonism.

This trend—apparently global—is what Bourdieu calls the strengthening of the so-called right hand of the state: macro-policies that reinforce material and moral misery through institutional means, giving rise, in our context, to more authoritarian criminal policies of surveillance and repression. Naturally, this comes at the expense of the left hand of the state, which is increasingly relegated, even forgotten, in its protective and supportive function.[10]

In sum, as the state's social function is obscured, its repressive function expands—to the point that the former becomes a vague hope, a distant light at the end of a tunnel that no one can see, though its existence is still asserted.

In such a scenario, the idea of nation—whether legally or sociologically understood—does not remain unscathed. For, in either case, it presupposes some measure of social unification (*reductio ad unum*), a minimal degree of fraternal linkage and shared meaning. This foundational idea is inseparable from equality: "It is obvious that the smaller the inequalities, the easier it will be to achieve social harmony, since the very notion of common good will be more easily established if all the people have the same cultural values. It is, therefore, convenient for the state to act to establish the maximum possible general rules for all the people."[11]

In other words, it is reaffirmed that the idea of a nation cannot be realized in a fragmented society—a society cleaved ever more clearly between a shrinking minority of the privileged and a growing majority of *pariahs*, regarded as socially unworthy and disposable.

3.3 The Caste State and Its Insurmountable Hierarchy of Humanity

The diagnosis of the growing distancing of the Rule of Law model in social reality is not difficult, as its most evident sign leaps out in the realm of *criminal issues*.

The high lethality of Brazilian punitive power, its broad selective capacity toward the most vulnerable segments, the inertia of the powers of the republic on this issue—especially the judiciary—the manipulation of these same powers by the media, the selfish corporatism of punitive agencies resulting in their increasing *atomization*, and the selection of crimes against property as the primary focus, considered collectively, clearly reveal the characteristics of a very pronounced—almost total—legal disorder in the exercise of punitive power. Undoubtedly, this is the most unmistakable sign—in any country—of the distancing of social reality from the normative objectives universally understood as constituting a Rule of Law.

In this context, it is obvious that the real standard of equality before the law is weakened to the extreme in Brazilian criminal practice, when it should instead be presumed that its constant elevation is a basic requirement of any true Rule of Law.

Punitivism manifests itself in the legal frameworks that program the primary criminalization of so-called subsistence delinquency—in particular, crimes against property—perfectly functional to the labeling of selected individuals from the supposed caste of pariahs, who are nothing more than the vast and growing majority excluded by the effects of structural social inequalities that, far from being alleviated, intensify.

This is the clearest sign that the state, moving in the opposite direction to that prescribed by its highest-ranking laws, distances the social being from the constitutional "ought to be," shaping a society in which, as has often been said ironically, some are more equal than others.

The disordered and even chaotic institutional panorama, in terms of the legal disorder of punitive power, serves only to weaken the foundations of democracy itself,[12] since any selective arbitrariness at the hands of autonomous agencies—or even of individuals outside the state structure—entails the consecration and deepening of discriminations that erode the most elementary democratic values. The result is the configuration of a state model that seems to consolidate itself and clearly reveals its complete divergence from the one prescribed by the constitutional charter.[13]

While it is alarming that Brazil is in a process of accelerated distancing from the Rule of Law model, with uncontrolled punitive power playing a central role,[14] the truth is that this regression—which could reach the point of general weakening of the state's most basic functions—has not yet reached that stage. Therefore, without unfounded optimism, we believe that it remains possible to stop and reverse it, starting from a proposal that at least aims to contain the current uncontrolled punitive impulse.

Any solution must begin with a correct diagnosis of the situation to be reversed and, above all, a precise understanding of its scale. In this sense, it is crucial to recognize that, in any country, the criminal issue is important but should occupy a relatively secondary place among the priorities and urgencies of society and, accordingly, of its state.

However, this is not the situation in the Brazilian context, where the legally and partially state-uncontrolled exercise of punitive power has assumed such a central dimension that it has become the key piece of the trend toward consolidating a sort of caste state, organized under the guiding idea that there are different *levels of citizens*[15]—almost like a worsened return to the Greek polis—which, for obvious reasons, is not admitted in political or media discourse. Yet, no great sociological insight is needed to realize that this guiding idea—or perhaps basic axiology—underlies, consciously or unconsciously, the pragmatic plane of legal, social, and political activity.

The all-too-frequent phenomenon of the discriminated adopting the values of the discriminator operates on an extraordinary social dimension, driven by monopolistic media. It leads the excluded and *marginalized* to participate in this particular "leveling." A simplistic but highly effective communicational tactic creates stereotypes and generates hatred among them. Through an unusual movement of psychosocial denial—of what truly is—they are made to believe that "the other," of the same social condition, is the "inferior," thus inventing a difference that makes them feel superior to the "pariah": "I am poor, but not a pariah"; and even more: "I am middle class, but not a worker."

It is not merely about making someone feel "superior" economically, which would be an illusion limited to material conditions; it is about defining the "pariah" as inferior as a human being (*Untermenschen*), worthy or deserving of death or any other sad fate. It is not about creating illusions about "social classes," which are crossable, but about hallucinating "castes," *which are uncrossable because they correspond to hierarchies of "humanity."*

Hallucinating the existence of an inferior caste of "lesser humans" allows the "others" to feel part of a supposed superior caste, safe from the hatred and repression directed at the "inferiors." Let us recall the old Lombrosian biologism, which reassured those who did not fit the stereotype of the "born criminal" because they were not organically inferior and thus were safe from the treatment reserved for the stereotyped—those likened to the colonized.[16]

It is clear that punitive power does not operate this way. It moves through stereotypes and very well-defined exclusionary objectives,[17] regardless of any subjective identification with one caste or another. The *distribution of immunity to punitive power* does not depend on the subjective perception of the individual,[18] who, despite feeling safe, is actually not; hence, those who are selected are taken by surprise, experiencing reactions of astonishment, disbelief, denial, and depression from feeling betrayed, as well as social resentment—reactions that often precipitate serious behavioral deviations.

The rejection of the supposed caste of "inferior humans" by the excluded themselves serves to politically and socially disorganize them, preventing any insurrection or critical gaze toward those above,[19] that is, toward the *plutophilic* minority that defines contemporary criminal policy.[20]

This is nothing but a perverse translation of the ancient tactic *divide et impera.*[21] As hatred toward the other excluded is cultivated, contradictions sharpen, and dialog is stifled, blocking the possibility of becoming aware of one's own exclusion.

It can be said, without much doubt, that this emerging caste state responds to the dynamics of a supposedly hierarchical rabble, completely antithetical to the merely discursive paradigm of equality before the law—which, clearly, is bereft of any minimal guiding value in the realm of social reality.

In a translation of the racist social imaginary, maximized by the media,[22] a citizenry distinction is practiced: full citizens (a privileged minority immune to punitive power), subcitizens (the working classes), and, finally, the caste of *pariahs*,[23] which comprises the majority of the population and is increasingly subjected to unlimited punitive power.

From a political-institutional perspective, all this is possible because, in this model of state power, the penal issue plays a decisive role in containing the expanding, excluded population.

The weakened, *labile Rule of Law*—whose fragility becomes ever more evident—lacks the capacity or power to contain the impulses of punitive power, relegating everything that pertains to human rights to the lowest priority. Institutional actors, faced with this, resign themselves, for they are the ones most affected by the dismantling of the state's protective power.

By action or omission, the powers of the state foster these impulses of punitive power against the excluded, failing to contain them legally and thereby allowing their expansion with increasingly lethal manifestations.

The absence of strong state authority, endowed with the institutional power of legal containment, leaves increasing room for arbitrary and violent exercises of punitive power, gradually demolishing every pretense of realizing the postulates of the democratic Rule of Law.

The inertia—at best—of state institutions in the face of the expansion of punitive power signals the very weakening of the state, enabling what has been called the *pluralization of punitive and collection systems*,[24] a renewed version of the parallel and *underground penal systems*[25] characteristic of the police states of Latin American national security dictatorships.[26]

However, there is a crucial difference: Under those dictatorships, although exercising wide arbitrary powers, the parallel systems remained subordinated to a political top—even if dictatorial. In contrast, today's punitive power is increasingly fragmented and lacks a strong political top that sets limits to its functionality.

At present, punitive power is in the hands of well-structured groups that control territories and even the penitentiary system, such as *militias in the favelas* or members of criminal organizations in the major cities' vulnerable communities, where the operative penal law is no longer that of the state but of whoever holds control. Nothing could more clearly signal the growing loss of sovereignty of the state, which, by losing its hegemony over the power to punish,[27] dilutes one of the very essences of modern statehood.

Thus, the panorama of the current context of punitive power demands the greatest intellectual efforts to devise tactics capable of containing its overflow—not merely as an elementary civilizing task to redirect institutions toward minimum respect for constitutionally enshrined international human rights, but because what is ultimately at stake is the reconstruction of the state itself, weakened not just as a Rule of Law but as a state proper.

Imagining a punitive power exercised with prudence means envisioning a state sufficiently capable of legally containing it. For our part, we firmly believe that this can only be a model as close as possible to the Social Rule of Law: one whose objective is the person, governed by a legal order that transcends any form of transpersonal idolatry and which, according to world experience, remains the only viable path to reducing discrimination and the symbolic or real hierarchies of caste.

In other words, it is the return to the ancient, indissoluble trinity of the Rule of Law: *liberty, equality, and fraternity*.

3.4 The Caste State and Its Anti-Model of Criminal Policy

The criminal policy of a state is never the product of mere chance or isolated historical events. Despite its occasional inconsistencies, it always reflects an institutional stance of an essentially political nature.[28] Each state consciously chooses the criminal policy it wishes to pursue—an orientation that cannot be entirely separated from the underlying model of the state from which it emerges, even if it admits deviations or nonessential variations.

However, this state model is not determined by its constitutional proclamations but rather by the way the state behaves in its institutional reality—that is, by the model it effectively operates in practice. This often diverges from the one it claims to uphold discursively.

These discrepancies may be superficial, since the ideal of a democratic Rule of Law is never fully realized. It serves more as a normative benchmark, a reference point to measure the extent of its actual implementation. In this light, the criminal policies of different real or historical Rule of Law states may differ in relatively moderate ways. But substantial, structural, and foundational divergences also exist—especially when, in practice, the state is not one governed by the Rule of Law, but merely one that invokes it as an *unfulfilled constitutional promise*. In such cases, we must ask: What kind of state is this in reality?

This is precisely the case in Brazil, where it becomes clear that the country's criminal policy is not democratic[29]—precisely because it does not stem from a model of a fully realized democratic state governed by the Rule of Law, but rather from a *caste state* that gives rise to a suicidal criminal policy, destructive even to the state itself.

This might seem like a truism, as it could not be otherwise: A democratic criminal policy must, by necessity, be guided by the principles of a state that materially approximates the democratic Rule of Law—not merely in *formal* or *discursive* terms, which, in the end, amount to nothing more than imaginary or *idealized* constructs.[30]

Under these conditions, the expected outcome of the current Brazilian state, in terms of criminal policy, can only be chaotic. It results in a real loss of control over the exercise of a fragmented punitive power, which, in practice, functions as the interlocking mechanisms of a machine designed to destroy the vulnerable and perpetuate violence.

In a dynamic of complementarity, defined by the criminal policy of the "other," the extremely high rates of lethality associated with punitive power—as discussed in the previous chapter—reveal a perverse preference for Black and Brown bodies, especially the young. This amounts to a true genocide in the country. It is no longer the *slow-drip genocide* once denounced by Latin American criminological critique in the last century,[31] but the full opening of the floodgates of extermination against the most vulnerable—those deemed inferior.[32]

We do not believe that the stark racial disparities in incarceration and lethality rates—both converging on a specific racial profile—are mere coincidences. An intellectually honest look at Brazil's punitive power and criminal policy makes it clear that these figures are not random; they reflect a deeply rooted structure of discrimination. Indeed, any serious researcher who approaches the issue from an interdisciplinary perspective would easily recognize the underlying logic that permeates the country's current criminal policy.

It is truly distressing to realize how far removed we are from the principles of an emancipatory criminal policy—one that promotes social peace, is grounded in sound scientific and technical knowledge, and operates within the strict boundaries established by the constitution. What we see instead is a criminal policy that flagrantly disregards rationality and fails to make even the slightest effort to adhere to constitutionally mandated limits.[33]

Our criminal policy—if it can even be called that—categorically rejects any initiative aimed at aligning with rationality. It locks itself into a trajectory that obstructs or neutralizes any action or reaction intended to correct the course of an extermination-and-exclusion model imposed upon historically constructed *pariahs* and *subcitizens*. To that end, every opportunity is seized to discredit any critical voice that might rise up against the model being actively consolidated.

Criticisms from academic sectors are either ignored or drowned out by the cacophony of television punditry and social media noise, amplified by false experts, unscrupulous politicians, and "omniscient" commentators whose supposed authority has recently extended beyond criminal matters to challenge even the world's leading scientific institutions—as occurred during the global COVID-19 pandemic.

The lack of political scruples—now magnified by the power of concentrated media and amplified through social networks—has forged a new reality. Until recently, this apparatus was content with concealing the thousands of corpses produced by unchecked punitive power. Now, *in an era of financial totalitarianism* that subjugates democracies to the interests of large transnational corporations,[34] it seeks to construct a "new democratic reality" that is, in truth, profoundly undemocratic. This fabrication is driven by fake news, post-truth narratives, and an extreme concentration of wealth—all methods that contribute to the erosion of state structures through every form of manipulation, including for electoral gain.

The previous stage was marked by contempt for the knowledge produced by sociologists and criminologists. The current stage goes even further: It seeks nothing less than to undermine the very principles that uphold the democratic Rule of Law. Reality, little by little, is "hitting bottom" under the weight of relentless media fabrication and the spread of social media hatred toward a despicable "other"—a figure meticulously constructed by the media, with whom no one wishes to identify.

In the academic sphere, we are witnessing a disturbing usurpation of scientific knowledge by immoral politicians, media conglomerates, and mercenaries posing as journalists. In this context, advertising supplants science, commercial *spots* replace scholarly texts, and irrationality triumphs over reason.[35]

Even within criminal law itself, academic discourse often retreats into theoretical constructs built upon epistemologies that block the incorporation of social realities. This *normativism* attempts to make us live in a world of norms rather than a world of things, confusing logic with ontology. Meanwhile, information drawn from sociology and the human sciences—which, by their very nature, tend to adopt critical perspectives in the face of the realities we denounce—is often dismissed as unscientific or reduced to mere "political" or "ideological" discourse. This reflects a supposed hierarchy of knowledge in which "true" science must be aseptic, as if the criminal question were somehow devoid of cultural, historical, and political substance.

It should be noted that this chaotic criminal policy also differs from that implemented—and criticized—in the so-called developed world. Although it shares certain features and functional convergences, these similarities are to be expected in a global order shaped by the *financialization* of the economy.[36]

This marked difference with the *Global North* can be explained by the geopolitical position of the region and, more specifically, by the historical and socioeconomic development of Brazil. These conditions are key factors behind a criminal policy that not only tolerates suffering but systematically produces it. In this sense, the enduring scars of racial discrimination and social inequality cannot be ignored. They help explain why Brazil's criminal policy *anti-model* is among the most lethal in the region.

If history is not merely the past, but rather what manifests in present-day consequences, then any researcher who overlooks the deep imprint left by the *slaveholding* system—and the chronological challenge it poses—will find it difficult to grasp the present state of Brazil's criminal policy. On the contrary, the persistent relevance of this historical wound becomes undeniable when analyzing the *profiles* of those who populate Brazil's deteriorated prison system: the direct descendants of more than two centuries of slavery, reconfigured in contemporary times through a refined *modus operandi* that continues to reproduce segregation.[37]

The *racial factor* not only shapes the political-criminal dynamic, leading to the high concentration of melanin in Brazil's overcrowded prisons, but it is also strikingly evident in the almost identical overrepresentation of Black and Brown individuals among the victims of lethal violence. As previously shown, the demographic profiles of those who fill the prisons and those who fall to violent deaths are practically indistinguishable.[38]

In short, to a large extent, Brazil's criminal policy is one of multiplying lethality. It selects, criminalizes, and targets poor, stereotyped young people from historically vulnerable groups. Initially, they appear in statistics as part of the mass incarceration for property-related offenses. But once they enter the prison system—degraded to the extreme and with a high criminogenic potential—they become absorbed into the cycle of violence and eventually swell the statistics of lethal crimes. This explains the striking correlation between imprisonment rates and violent deaths, as well as the shared characteristics of both populations: The overlap is not accidental but rather the outcome of a deadly criminal policy.

Within this dynamic, the high percentage of pretrial detainees in the prison population reflects the normalization of preventive detention in judicial practice. Following trends seen in other countries in the region, it is often applied as a form of anticipated punishment.[39] As in the general incarceration data, these provisional detentions overwhelmingly involve alleged property crimes and other offenses of minor legal significance—what is commonly referred to as *subsistence delinquency*.

Despite this incontrovertible reality, clearly evidenced by official data, mainstream media propaganda continues to defend the indiscriminate use of preventive detention—an approach that blatantly violates sound procedural principles. With the support of certain judges whose conduct deviates from institutional norms, this practice is promoted as a powerful tool against crimes committed by privileged social classes. Yet, this portrayal is just another fallacy of punitivism, which—as is well known—lacks any commitment to intellectual honesty in its construction of reality.

The panorama of this suicidal criminal policy is, as we have already stated, distinct from that of the *Global North* and even from other countries in our own region. It is as desolate as it is undeniable: a vicious cycle of lethality specifically targeting vulnerable youth. These young people are, of course, systematically excluded from the classrooms of the country's top universities—historically reserved for white elites[40]—and instead funneled into overcrowded prisons, where they become agents in the reproduction of violence and, ultimately, victims of repressive lethality.

The panorama of chaotic criminal policy in Brazil would be incomplete without mention of the phenomenon of police autonomy, which represents the first crucial step toward the loss of control over punitive power in any country in the region. As elsewhere, autonomous police forces begin to raise funds outside the formal systems of taxation and public service fees. To do so, they must establish extortionist or coercive mechanisms while simultaneously legitimizing themselves before the public—often through media narratives that construct the illusion of a "war on crime." In practice, this war is sustained by the lethal targeting of vulnerable youth. The result is the existence of *parallel* systems of revenue collection and punitive power, operating entirely outside institutional frameworks.

This results in a dizzying increase in police lethality,[41] which—as we have already emphasized—serves a dual purpose: On the one hand, it secures the autonomy of police revenue; on the other hand, it sustains their image as socially useful institutions. The latter is achieved through the massive secondary selection of media stereotypes drawn from a racist social imaginary. These stereotypes, in turn, justify the extraordinarily high levels of violence inflicted upon the vulnerable, thereby reinforcing the warlike image that legitimizes police action in the eyes of the public.

As we have just pointed out, this criminal policy is deeply intertwined with the media-driven construction of a war narrative—one shaped by converging paranoid elements that give rise to the invented figure of the pariah, held responsible for all societal ills. This *warlike image* is constantly reinforced by monopolized media propaganda, which manufactures a single version of reality. In doing so, it amplifies prejudices and resentments that are socially entrenched and historically conditioned. In Brazil, as elsewhere, *punitivism* feeds on these sentiments and pushes them further—employing the same perverse political method historically used to legitimize genocides, as seen throughout human history and most notoriously in the darkest episodes of the last century.

These prejudices—which should, of course, be challenged in any democratic and pluralistic society—are, in Brazil, instead reaffirmed and nourished by concentrated media. These outlets manipulate public opinion, deepening the internalization of such prejudices into the collective value system. Over time, these prejudices become the very foundation of criminal policy discourse, ultimately assuming the character of an official state policy.

From this *warlike perspective*, the notion that "the only good criminal is a dead criminal" becomes a legitimized maxim. In the paranoid social imaginary constructed by concentrated media, the *caste of pariahs* is portrayed as the embodiment of all the vices and defects of Brazilian society. Those assigned to this caste—the so-called criminals—are represented as a subclass of human beings, scapegoated for the nation's problems. They are perceived as a constant threat to the very *status of personhood*, which must, in turn, be reaffirmed daily through the repeated denial of that same status to the pariahs.

3.5 Who are the Pariahs?

The war on the *pariahs*—like every war metaphor introduced into the social imaginary and lived as reality—has historically served to legitimize the unrestricted exercise of punitive power by fabricating a fearsome enemy who is desired dead. From the persecution of *witches*[42] and the inquisition to the ideology of *national security*,[43] this logic has remained constant. This is the well-known process of demonization, which is, in the end, somewhat redundant: "Satan," in Hebrew, means enemy. Thus, demonization would literally become "enemization"[44]—an awkward neologism in Spanish.

But we must ask: Does this *creation of an enemy* merely assign that condition, as a qualifier, to a real social group? This question is a key to understanding the functioning of the Brazilian caste state. The curious—and at the same time revealing—aspect of this tactic's perversity is that there is, in fact, no group that identifies itself as *pariahs*. Labeling all socially marginalized groups as *pariahs* would be only partially accurate, since their vulnerability does not automatically translate into that status.

In societies where this negative phenomenon is absent, it is difficult to grasp—and even within societies afflicted by it, the phenomenon is often not clearly perceived, as it may initially seem contradictory.

The closest analytical tool offered by social science comes from the Brazilian sociologist Jessé Souza.[45] Drawing on Max Weber, Souza argues that the function of the pariah caste in India lies in enabling everyone else *to feel superior*. In non-caste-based societies, a similar dynamic is fabricated: A media-invented *caste of pariahs* is constructed to concentrate the most negative, discriminatory prejudices of the society. This, in turn, produces a phenomenon we mentioned earlier: the excluded distancing themselves from the *pariahs*.

3.6 But Do Pariahs Exist or Not Exist?

The well-known *Thomas theorem*[46] provides the key to this question: It matters little whether pariahs truly exist—if their existence is taken for granted, the consequences are real, and *pariahs* come into being. They are nothing more than vulnerable young people selected or executed by punitive power, to whom the status of "pariah" is attributed so that the other excluded groups may distance themselves and feel superior—until one of them, or their children, is eventually selected and victimized by the same punitive machinery.

This is a media-driven construction in which the logic of the *Thomas theorem* operates perfectly and on a massive scale. In truth, *pariahs exist only potentially*: They are all the vulnerable members of society who, at any moment, may be designated as such by the same concentrated media that *invent the caste*. Yet, until they are victimized, these individuals perceive themselves as unrelated to that status. They internalize the values of the discriminatory discourse and feel protected from the very punitive power they help legitimize through everyday interactions—until, numbed by the hallucinated war, they begin to see such violence as *normal*.

There is, however, another element that must be taken seriously: the unequal social distribution of the risk of victimization, which remains selective in every society. Those most vulnerable to victimization also belong to the most disadvantaged social classes. The vulnerability of the excluded lies not only in their exposure to criminalization but also in their heightened risk of becoming victims[47]—particularly in a society that tends to *privatize public services*, including, unsurprisingly, security itself, in accordance with a generalized logic of *meritocracy*.[48]

This explains the social permeability of what we might call a *criminal policy of the other*—a model that directs its repressive gaze toward an "other" with whom no one wishes to identify and who is portrayed as the primary cause of crime, in a kind of regression to *Lombrosian determinism*.

Thus, the very people who are *potential pariahs* distance themselves from that identity when the figure of the criminal is painted as the "bad guy," adorned with features that describe no real social group but instead result from the perverse amplification of prejudice. These traits, embedded in media-constructed criminal stereotypes, circulate widely through the channels of concentrated propaganda.[49]

3.7 Neither Right nor Left: The Political-Criminal Dynamics of the Advanced Phase of Criminal Selectivity

The macro- and micro-social dynamics of this criminal policy converge in what we may call the *advanced phase of criminal selectivity*. This stage is marked by both the lethality of punitive power and the phenomenon of mass incarceration—each institutionalized through state policies. This leads us to the conclusion that the current depth of criminal selectivity in Brazil—now truly abyssal—can be explained as the outcome of a structural omission in criminal policy sustained over decades.

It is an omission rooted in a deliberate historical amnesia—one that denies the very foundations of our society: a past built on racism, social exclusion, and the enslavement of Black and Brown bodies.[50] These structures have never been fully overcome, neither in daily life nor, even less so, in the collective imagination.[51] It is, in essence, the assertion of a false narrative that Brazil has left behind the stain of exploitation and is now marching toward a supposedly harmonious and *ethnically* diverse coexistence.[52]

This omission—or rather, this denialism—consists of refusing to confront reality under the guise of a false belief that it has already been overcome. Its consequence has been the deepening of social distances, the entrenchment of prejudices and stereotypes, and the neutralization of any sufficiently sensitive and effective political or social response to the open use of punitive power as a mechanism for continuing the segregationist logic that has always played a central role in Brazil's institutional and social structures.

Denial, in individual psychology, is a mechanism for escaping a troubling or conflict-ridden reality. While individual psychological mechanisms cannot be transferred directly to the social sphere, neither can they be entirely disregarded.

In this case, the collective "escape from reality" has led to a serious political omission: a failure to confront the advance of uncontrolled punitive power.

The truth is that a significant current within criminal policy—one aimed at restraining the impulses of punitive power—was never genuinely promoted in Brazil. On the contrary, everything suggests that such impulses have been encouraged, allowing punitive power to expand without limits over those who are always undesirable, already symbolically clothed in the status of pariahs.

The state's criminal policy lacks any realistic understanding of the penal issue. It is distorted by biased portrayals and the dissemination of manipulated data by the media—yet it manages to convince the population, particularly the most socioeconomically vulnerable, of the supposed need for greater punitive power, which will inevitably be exercised against them. This strategy ends up shaping government programs, which adopt increasingly punitive measures in order to gain or retain voter support.[53]

In this way, governments become both accomplices and hostages of the media's construction of reality, insofar as the major communication monopolies succeed in establishing a kind of public consensus around a perverse and selective punitive vision of criminality[54]—one that operates entirely detached from any critical or reflective knowledge.

This complex process fuels the exercise of unchecked punitive power and the lethal violence inherent in it, resulting in a persistent and forceful obstruction of any attempt to implement even a minimally democratic criminal policy. It often seems as though the dominant power structures—through their principal spokespersons, the major media monopolies—act deliberately to block any criminal policy initiative that might lead to even the slightest control over punitive power.

In recent decades, we have witnessed the rise of opportunistic politicians—false outsiders—who exploit the criminal issue and *vindictive punitivism* to gain access to the popular imagination. This imagination is partly manipulated by concentrated media and partly shaped by deeply rooted structures of racism and classism. These politicians shamelessly capitalize on prejudices and collective fears to secure popular support, which ultimately translates into votes.[55]

However, the investment in punitive demagoguery—which distorts reality and operates as a form of *denialism* in the face of the extensive evidence historically produced by penal and criminological research—has not been exclusive to any one political or ideological spectrum in Brazil. All shades of political orientation have, to varying degrees, embraced this hate-driven criminal policy. Its key indicators—rising lethality and mass incarceration—have only intensified across successive governments.

From a logic detached from empirical reality and based purely on ideology, one might assume that such a criminal policy is the direct result of politically conservative governments—in other words, of the so-called political and neoliberal right, much like the initial impulses behind "law and order" or "citizen security" policies around the world.[56] However, reality reveals that this is a mistaken assumption, rooted in ideological bias.

In Brazil, the lines separating right and left are blurred. Political leaders and parties—both in their histories and in their practices, whether in power or in opposition—have demonstrated that no direct coherence exists that would allow for a clear-cut, enlightenment-style dichotomy.[57] Brazil presents a true political spectrum, with a multitude of shifting actions and positions that follow a pendular logic. This forces us to rethink and practically resignify the traditional notion of right and left in the Brazilian context.

This does not mean that we must entirely discard the dichotomy between right and left. On the contrary, it remains a useful analytical tool for locating, within the ideological spectrum, where Brazil's criminal policy of recent decades might be situated—especially when considering prospects for correcting or redirecting its trajectory. In this sense, the more promising paths appear to emerge when perspectives generally regarded as progressive in the broader social field come into play.

Using the idea of equality as the backbone of the distinction between the two ideological positions,[58] we might say that those who identify with the left tend to place greater emphasis—in both moral conduct and political action—on what makes people equal or on ways of reducing inequalities. Conversely, those who identify with the right generally believe that inequalities are inevitable and that their elimination is neither realistic nor desirable.[59] In this view, inequality is naturalized—almost consecrated—as a sort of immutable right, thus legitimizing, quite conveniently, their condition as oppressors.

Thus, this latter political stance within the broader ideological spectrum serves as the foundation for the *criminal policy of blood and pain* that has been practiced in recent decades. Through the unchecked expansion of punitive power, it does nothing but reinforce and consolidate the structural social inequalities that underpin Brazilian society.

The above underscores the contradictions of political projects aligned with the left—or, more precisely, those considered progressive—which, in the realm of criminal policy, have adopted positions entirely at odds with their supposed commitment to promoting equality or reducing inequality. In other words, they have implemented and even intensified the same lethal criminal policies traditionally associated with conservative political forces. This is clearly reflected in the Brazilian political landscape of recent decades, which has been predominantly governed by the so-called progressive field.

Therefore, it must be concluded that, in terms of criminal policy, Brazil offers no clear distinction between what is commonly referred to—purely for didactic purposes—as left and right. Both camps have developed or tolerated the same genocidal criminal policy. Within the progressive field, a segment of the left continues to place its faith in criminalization as a tool for addressing structural social issues such as poverty, racism, gender violence, and LGBTIQ-phobia. This position has come to be known as the *punitive left*.[60]

The main distinction between these two perspectives lies in the progressive field's commitment to a less unjust distribution of income and a significant reduction in social inequality—an approach consistent with the traditional stance of the left. However, this policy was incoherently accompanied by a repeated willingness to comply with the punitive demands of media monopolies. On the one hand, the living standards of vulnerable populations improved; on the other hand, imprisonment and lethality rates affecting those same populations soared. This paradox reveals a kind of *bipolar or schizophrenic disorder within national politics*—one that has cost, and continues to cost, many lives.

This demonstrates that there is no causal relationship between rising income levels and reductions in incarceration and lethality rates.[61] Expanding real citizenship is merely one strand—perhaps the most important—within a much broader web of factors needed to restrain the exercise of punitive power. Undoubtedly, this thread must be accompanied by an active criminal policy commitment aimed at fostering such containment.

In summary, it must be clear that the political-criminal dynamics of the advanced phase of penal selectivity in Brazil are not the result of a single government or political group. This deterioration in criminal policy is transversal; it has effectively become a state policy carried out by governments of all ideological stripes since at least the period of redemocratization. One could say that, in Brazil, there is not a criminal policy of governments, but rather a criminal policy of the state—one that systematically undermines the very foundations of the democratic state. It is, in essence, *a criminal policy of self-cannibalism.*

3.8 Beyond Harmony: For an Interdisciplinary Convergence Between Powers

As a first step in any meaningful proposal, the relationship between law and politics must be clarified, thus overcoming the false antagonism between the legal and the political. Law—whether in the form of legislation, jurisdictional activity, or legal science—contributes, directly or indirectly, to the governance of the *polis*, that is, to the political sphere.[62] If legal science aspires to become jurisprudence, then each judicial decision constitutes an act of government, as it emanates from one of the powers of the state.

The false antagonism between these two spheres is a lingering inheritance from traditional modes of thought, if not a rationalized excuse for shirking responsibilities—whose negative effects are repeatedly and emphatically manifested in the field of criminal law. The first legal framework that the criminal law scholar must integrate into their theoretical constructions is the constitution itself; evidently, a constitution is nothing less than the *political code* of a state.

To postulate or assume a watertight separation between the political and the legal implies, among other things, a denial of reality's complexity and a refusal to acknowledge that the intersection between these fields entails a relationship of reciprocal complementarity. This does not entail abandoning technique—for every politics requires a technique—but rather demands a clear and intellectually honest rethinking of the epistemological boundaries between law and politics.[63] In the end, this is nothing more than recognizing a basic *logisch-objektiv* fact: Beyond being technical, law is political.

When the two domains are scrupulously separated—allegedly to guarantee the "scientific" and rational nature of law—one follows a flawed methodological path, one that is not only idealistic but ultimately arbitrary. Rationality, in fact, requires that the boundaries and interactions between law and politics be explicitly acknowledged. For, by a paradox that is as inevitable as it is revealing, asserting that such limits are insurmountable only results in confusing them—thereby disguising politics as "apolitical."

This occurs because law, being inherently political, cannot be rendered "nonpolitical" without denying its very nature. Any such pretense refers to something impossible and, thus, nonexistent. What results, in truth, is purely political or ideological activity that seeks to legitimize itself under the guise of legal science.

When one proceeds along this erroneous path, not only is the political content of legal knowledge denied, but—given that such knowledge is intended for legal operators—the political dimension of the judiciary itself is also obscured. As a branch of state power, the judiciary can never cease to be political.[64] This does not entail a loss of rationality; on the contrary, it affirms the very rationality imposed by the republican principle upon all acts of government—a rationality that can only be recognized and evaluated once its veil of so-called neutrality and political asepsis is lifted.

Having clarified the above, any effort aimed at reducing selectivity in the exercise of punitive power—and at advancing the realization of the principles of the Rule of Law—has an unmistakable and well-defined political character. Moreover, it demands a coherent and coordinated intervention from all branches of the republic.

This joint intervention must necessarily entail a convergence of efforts that goes far beyond the traditional notion of harmony historically enshrined and characteristic of contemporary democracies. Understanding that this is a central issue for the nation's destiny demands that, in order to achieve the dual objective of reducing selectivity and advancing the Rule of Law, the relationship between the branches of government must be renewed—not through unnecessary innovations, but through a firm commitment to aligning their actions with the new and complex demands of containing a punitive power that operates without control and is, in part, external to institutional authority, as a consequence of the very degradation of the state.

This joint effort—which must be driven by a healthy sense of national purpose—is both indispensable and distinct from what is commonly referred to as "harmony" between powers, which often amounts to little more than empty rhetoric. In the day-to-day life of our deteriorated democracy, such harmony is reduced, at best, to a minimal level of "tolerance" among branches of government or, in more fortunate cases, a merely necessary form of mutual respect.

While harmony presupposes much more than mere respect or tolerance—since it implies cooperation—carrying out this endeavor, which ultimately aims to reclaim the attributes of sovereignty and elevate the standards of the constitutional

Rule of Law, demands *strong and coherent collaboration* animated by a high vocation of service to the nation itself.

Obviously, respecting the boundaries of each branch of government is essential, as failing to do so would undermine their respective independence—one of the pillars of any modern republican and democratic order. Therefore, the kind of cooperation being proposed here has nothing to do with overstepping the constitutional limits assigned to each power. It is by no means about erasing the lines that delineate the competencies of the judiciary, the legislature, or the executive—much less merging them.

Cooperation is needed in the sense of a foundational agreement based on a shared objective, with each branch acting within its constitutional scope but collectively oriented toward safeguarding the very survival of the republican powers. It is about restoring part of their lost competence, recovering the strength of the state and the principles of the constitutional model, in response to a national demand confronted by the catastrophic consequences of the country's abysmal legal-penal selectivity.

It is both indispensable and urgent to define clear strategic objectives, which can only be: to restore the hegemony of the state's fiscal and punitive powers, to exercise the former equitably, and to contain the latter within rational boundaries as close as possible to the constitutional Rule of Law. The strategies adopted by each branch of government, within their respective areas of competence, must be urgently reoriented in this direction—as part of a convergence of efforts aligned toward a common goal.

Given the complexity, magnitude, and conflicting interests involved in any attempt to structurally reform the state's criminal policy, this cannot be a task successfully undertaken by a single branch of government. The transformation required exceeds the capacities of any isolated institutional actor.

The current *criminal policy of the other*, manifested in the abysmal and violent selectivity in the exercise of punitive power—which floods the country with dead and imprisoned vulnerable individuals, selected according to stereotypes fueled by discriminatory prejudices rooted in unhealed historical wounds—is steadily weakening the state. A convergence of efforts among the branches of government is the only viable institutional path to attempt to close the gates to this uncontrolled punitive power. Otherwise, we will continue accelerating toward the complete hollowing out of the Rule of Law and the deepening of the caste state that is gradually replacing it.

The concerted efforts of the state's branches toward a common strategic objective will require each of them to draw upon the disciplines most aligned and functional to their respective spheres of competence. Therefore, such a convergence of efforts would necessarily take the form of an interdisciplinary undertaking.

In short, no single discipline possesses all the heuristic tools sufficiently suited to analyze and address complex problems—the hallmark of today's hypercomplex society.[65] Nor does any isolated branch of government possess the necessary competence to overcome the abyssal penal selectivity—which would mean reversing the current criminal policy—precisely because it is a by-product of that same hypercomplex social structure.

In this sense, it is important to recognize that what is commonly referred to as the "penal system" is composed of segments that do not fall under the authority of a single branch of government—and not all of them are even state-owned.[66]

Thus, the penal system comprises, at a minimum: political agencies (executive and legislative), executive bodies (police), judicial operators, penitentiary institutions, advertising apparatuses (media), and ideological reproduction agencies (universities and academic institutions in general)[67]—not to mention the parallel punitive power, over which the state has lost its hegemony.

Each of these segments develops its own mores (internal culture), discourses (both internal and external), legitimations, and its own criteria of effectiveness, which lead to a certain degree of *fragmentation*—meaning that no single actor bears sole responsibility for the outcome of the whole. In the case of Brazil, this *fragmentation* reaches an extreme degree.

There are many signs of this extreme, but the most undeniable and evident is the issuance of penal sentences—especially pretrial detention orders, which are materially equivalent to sentences—by the judiciary without any consideration for the current prison conditions in the country, under the assumption that prison matters are the exclusive responsibility of the executive branch. This rationale exempts the judiciary from factoring in this concrete reality when issuing sentences. Hence, absurd the phenomenon of hundreds of thousands of unexecuted arrest warrants, simply because it is not possible to carry them out due to the overpopulation of prisoners.[68]

3.9 When Punishment Devours Democracy: A Self-Devouring Criminal Policy

All efforts aimed at overcoming the current criminal policy of the "other" cannot help but—through a kind of cause-and-effect relationship—lead to the strengthening of the democratic Rule of Law. In such a model, a punitive power that extends beyond situations of conflict in which it is strictly necessary is simply inadmissible. Therefore, this model must include the containment of those overflowing impulses—potentially and eventually genocidal—that are inherent to any *punitive power exercised without sufficient restraint.*

The current weakening of the Brazilian state is inseparable from its lack of control over the exercise of punitive power, as fostered by a *self-devouring criminal policy*. Consequently, any proposal to overcome this policy—even if it seems limited to the criminological field—inevitably implies the strengthening of the state itself and, in particular, of the democratic Rule of Law model. It therefore becomes a matter that far exceeds the scope of our discipline, transforming into a proposal that directly touches the very idea of the nation—an idea increasingly compromised by the disintegrative conflictivity nourished and intensified by the current criminal policy.

Only through the effective implementation of constitutional norms, and of strong and genuinely democratic institutions committed to seriously fulfilling the objectives set by the most basic principles of republican rationality, will it be possible to reverse the ongoing process of increasing *criminalizing selectivity* and the punitive violence characteristic of the current *criminal policy of the other.*

This criminal policy, characterized by the denial of the other—a fictitious othering fabricated by the media—strips individuals from vulnerable groups of their personhood, turning them into the primary targets of the *abysmal selectivity of punitive power.* This selectivity is fueled by racist stereotypes that converge upon the Black and mulatto populations of the country.

Overcoming this criminogenic policy—characteristic of the current caste state in which we are immersed—not only signals a departure from the constitutionally promised Rule of Law (a promise unkept), but also reveals the weakening, through the instrumentalization of the criminal issue, of the very idea of social unification (*reductio ad unum*).

This criminal policy has prevailed under the most diverse governments and ideological currents in recent decades. It could thus be said that it is not exclusive to a single sector of the ideological spectrum—left or right. Unlike what traditionally occurred in the political economy of punishment, these lines have become undeniably blurred, especially with the rise of the so-called *punitive left*, which, through action or omission, actively or passively contributes to the advancement of this policy. Moreover, its dynamics are perennial and transversal, constituting a state criminal policy oriented toward the weakening of the very democratic Rule of Law—thereby revealing the self-devouring nature of the criminal policy of the other.

Notes

1. Feuerbach, P. J. A. (1800). *Revision der Grundsätze und Grundbegriffe des positiven peinlichen Rechts*. Band 2. Erfurt: Georg Friedrich Tasché, p. 231.
2. Dworkin, R. (1989). *Los derechos en serio*. Barcelona: Editorial Ariel, pp. 31 ff.; Neves, M. (2013). *Entre Hidra e Hércules: Princípios e regras constitucionais como diferença paradoxal do sistema jurídico*. São Paulo: Martins Fontes, pp. 89 ff.; Alexy, R. (1993). *Teoría de los derechos fundamentales*. Madrid: Centro de Estudios Constitucionales, pp. 86 ff.
3. Wolfgang Sarlet, I. (2010). A eficácia dos direitos fundamentais: uma teoria geral dos direitos fundamentais na perspectiva constitucional. Porto Alegre: Livraria do Advogado Editora, pp. 459–460.
4. Gomes Canotilho, J. J. (2003). *Direito constitucional e teoria da constituição*. Coimbra: Almedina, pp. 1176 ff.
5. Bandeira de Mello, C. A. (2011). *O conteúdo jurídico do princípio da igualdade*. São Paulo: Malheiros Editores, pp. 9 ff.
6. Ferrajoli, L. (2019). *Manifesto per l'uguaglianza*. Roma: Laterza, pp. 10 ff.
7. Instituto Brasileiro de Geografia e Estatística. (2019). *Síntese de indicadores sociais: Uma análise das condições de vida da sociedade brasileira contemporânea*. Rio de

Janeiro: IBGE, pp. 6 ff.;Piketty, T. (2014). *El capital en el siglo XXI*. Madrid: Fondo de Cultura Económica, pp. 15 ff.;Piketty, T. (2015). *La economía de las desigualdades: Cómo implementar una redistribución justa y eficaz de la riqueza*. Buenos Aires: Siglo Veintiuno Editores, pp. 9 ff.

8. Neves, M. (1994). *A constitucionalização simbólica*. São Paulo: Editora Acadêmica, pp. 11 ff.
9. Gil Villa, F. (2013). *Introducción a las teorías criminológicas. Por qué rompemos con la norma*. Madrid: Tecnos, pp. 130 ff.
10. Bourdieu, P. (1993). *La misère du monde*. Paris: Éditions du Seuil, p. 222.
11. Dallari, D. A. (2016). *Elementos de teoria geral do Estado*. São Paulo: Saraiva, pp. 135–136.
12. Stiglitz, J. (2012). *El precio de la desigualdad: El 1 por ciento de la población tiene lo que el 99 por ciento necesita*. Madrid: Taurus, pp. 342 ff.; Stiglitz, J. (2018). *Globalization and Its Discontents Revisited: Anti-Globalization in the Era of Trump*. New York: Norton & Company, pp. 8 ff.; Stiglitz, J. (2007). *Making Globalization Work*. New York: Norton & Company, pp. 50 ff.
13. Bobbio, N., Matteucci, N., & Pasquino, G. (1983). *Dizionario di politica*. Torino: UTET, pp. 1141 ff.
14. Tavares, J. (1997). A crescente legislação penal e os discursos de emergência. *Discursos Sediciosos: Crime, Direito e Sociedade*, n. 4, v. 2, pp. 44 ff.
15. On this concept, although used in another historical context, see: Bobbio, N. (2020). *Eguaglianza e libertà*. Torino: Einaudi, p. 20.
16. Lombroso, C. (1884). *L'uomo delinquente in rapporto all'antropologia, giurisprudenza ed alle discipline carcerarie. Delinquente nato e pazzo morale*, terza edizione completamente rifatta con 17 tavole e 8 figure nel testo. Torino: Fratelli Bocca, p. 248, argued that "in general, most of the born-criminals have looped ears, abundant hair, prominent frontal sinuses, huge jaw, square and protruding chin, widened cheekbones, frequent gesticulation, in short, a type resembling the Mongolic and sometimes the Negroid".
17. Pepino, L. (2012). *Forti con i deboli*. Milano: Bur, pp. 18 ff.
18. Ruggiero, V. (2013). *I crimini dell'economia: una lettura criminologica del pensiero economico*. Milano: Feltrinelli Editore, pp. 23 ff.
19. Sousa Santos, B. (2018). *Esquerdas do mundo, uni-vos*. São Paulo: Boitempo, pp. 31 ff.
20. Terradillos Basoco, J. M. (2020). *Aporofobia y plutofilia: La deriva jánica de la política criminal contemporánea*. Barcelona: Bosch Editor, pp. 27 ff.
21. Machiavelli, N. (2019). *Il Principe*. Milano: Feltrinelli Editore, p. 197, note 2.
22. Moreira, A. (2019). *Racismo recreativo*. São Paulo: Pólen, pp. 66 ff.
23. Souza, J. (2018). *Subcidadania brasileira: para entender o país além do jeitinho brasileiro*. Rio de Janeiro: Leya, pp. 34 ff.
24. Londoño Berrío, H. L. (2016). *Sistemas punitivos y derechos humanos: el caso de la Comuna 13 de Medellín—Colombia*. Bogotá: Ediciones Jurídicas Andrés Morales, pp. 23 ff.
25. Aniyar de Castro, L. (1987). *Criminología de la liberación*. Maracaibo: Editorial de la Universidad del Zulia, pp. 96 ff.
26. On the national security dictatorship in Brazil, see: Berdugo Gómez de la Torre, I. (2017). *La justicia transicional en Brasil. El caso de la guerrilla de Araguaia*. Salamanca: Ediciones Universidad de Salamanca, pp. 43 ff.
27. Beccaria, C. (1964). *Dei delitti e delle pene*. Facsimile dell'edizione originale pubblicata anonima in Livorno nel 1764 con le aggiunte delle successive edizioni e degli autografi registrate in margine e su carte allegate dal marchese Giulio Beccaria, figlio dell'Autore. Torino: Utet, pp. 23 ff.
28. Torrente, D. (2001). *Desviación y delito*. Madrid: Alianza Editorial, p. 84.; Moccia, S. (2002). Sul difficile rapporto tra principio di sussidiarietà, diritti fondamentali e politica criminali agli albori della postmodernità. *Diritti dell'uomo e sistema penale, vol. I*. Napoli: Edizioni Scientifiche Italiane, p. 123.; Calvo García, M. (1994). *Los fundamentos del método jurídico: una revisión crítica*. Madrid: Editorial Tecnos, pp. 279 ff.

29. Zúñiga Rodríguez, L. (2001). *Política criminal*. Madrid: Colex, pp. 19 ff.
30. Blanco Lozano, C. (2007). *Tratado de política criminal. Tomo I: Fundamentos científicos y metodológicos de la lucha contra el delito*. Barcelona: Bosch Editor, pp. 155 ff.; Sánchez-Ostiz, P. (2012). *Fundamentos de política criminal: un retorno a los principios*. Madrid: Marcial Pons, pp. 87 ff.
31. Zaffaroni, R. (2010). *Crímenes de masa*. Buenos Aires: Ediciones Madres de Plaza de Mayo, pp. 27 ff.
32. Along similar lines, Oliveira Pires, T. R. (2017). Criminologia crítica e pacto narcísico: por uma crítica criminológica apreensível em pretuguês. *Revista Brasileira de Ciências Criminais*, v. 135, 25, p. 557.; Do Nascimento, A. (1978). *O genocídio do negro brasileiro. Processo de um racismo mascarado*. Rio de Janeiro: Paz e Terra, pp. 41 ff.
33. Demetrio Crespo, E. (2020). *El derecho penal del Estado de derecho entre el espíritu de nuestro tiempo y la Constitución*. Madrid: Reus, pp. 109 ff.; Mir Puig, S. (2011). *Bases constitucionales del derecho penal*. Madrid: Iustel, pp. 58 ff.; Arroyo Zapatero, L. (1987). Fundamento y función del sistema penal: el programa penal de la Constitución. *Revista Jurídica de Castilla—La Mancha*, n. 1, pp. 97 ff.
34. Zaffaroni, R. & Dias dos Santos, Í. (2020). *La nueva crítica criminológica. Criminología en tiempos de totalitarismo financiero*. Valencia: Tirant lo Blanch.
35. Morin, E. (2020). *Changeons de voie: Les leçons du coronavirus* (avec la colaboración de Sabah Abouessalam). Paris: Éditions Denoël, pp. 69 ff.
36. Wacquant, L. (2007). *Parias urbains: ghetto, banlieues, État*. Paris: La Découverte.; Garland, D. (2011). *The culture of control. Crime and social order in contemporary society*. New York: Oxford University Press, pp. 12 ff.; Brandariz García, J. Á. (2014). *El gobierno de la penalidad. La complejidad de la política criminal contemporánea*. Madrid: Editorial Dykinson, pp. 75 ff.
37. Brandão, C. (2019). Poder e seletividade: Os processos de criminalização na América Latina e os seus impactos na crise do discurso penal. *Caderno de Relações Internacionais*, n. 18, v. 10, p. 36.
38. Graef, B. (2023). Onde mora a impunidade? Porque o Brasil precisa de um Indicador Nacional de Esclarecimento de Homicídios. *Instituto Sou da Paz*, São Paulo.
39. Neppi Modona, G. & Pelissero, M. (1997). La politica criminale durante il fascismo. In Violante, L. (a cura di), *Storia d'Italia. Annali 12. La criminalità*. Torino: Einaudi, pp. 829–830.
40. For an ethnographic description in this sense, see Dias Dos Santos, Í. (2017). Observatório da vida estudantil. Três itinerários de pesquisa: I. In Santos, G. G. dos, Vasconcelos, L. & Sampaio, S. M. R. (Dirs.), *Observatório da vida estudantil. Dez anos de estudos sobre vida e cultura universitária*. Salvador: Edufba, pp. 271–279.
41. Bechara, A. E. L. S. (2015). As mortes sem pena no Brasil: a difícil convergência entre Direitos Humanos, política criminal e Segurança Pública. *Revista da Faculdade de Direito da Universidade de São Paulo*, v. 110, pp. 21.
42. Kramer, H. & Sprenger, J. (2004). *Malleus Maleficarum: El martillo de las brujas. Para golpear a las brujas y sus herejías con poderosa maza*. Valladolid: Maxtor, pp. 35–196.
43. Berdugo Gómez de la Torre, I. *La justicia transicional en Brasil. El caso de la guerrilla de Araguaia*. Salamanca: Ediciones Universidad de Salamanca, pp. 43 ff.
44. Spee, F. (2017). *Cautio Criminalis: Cautela Criminal*. Buenos Aires: Ediar, pp. 13 ff.
45. Souza, J. (2017). *A elite do atraso: da escravidão à Lava Jato*. Rio de Janeiro: Leya, pp. 36 ff.; Souza, J. et al. (2018). *A ralé brasileira: quem é e como vive*. São Paulo: Editora Contracorrente, pp. 13 ff.
46. Thomas, W. I. & Thomas, D. S. (1928). *The child in America: behavior problems and programs*. New York: Knopf, p. 572.
47. Bustos Ramírez, J. & Larrauri, E. (1993). *Victimología: presente y futuro. Hacia un sistema penal de alternativas*. Barcelona: PPU, p. 80.; Tamarit Sumalla, J. M., Pereda, N. & Salinero, S. (2013). La victimización de las personas inmigrantes. In Pereda Beltran, N. & Tamarit

Sumalla, J. M. (Dirs.), *Victimología teórica y aplicada*. Barcelona: Huygens Editorial, p. 283.; Del Mar Daza Bonachela, M. (2016). *Escuchar a las víctimas. Victimología, Derecho victimal y atención a las víctimas*. Valencia: Tirant lo Blanch, p. 108.; Saad-Diniz, E. & Bessoni Boudoux Salgado, A. (2018). Violencia y victimización como costos sociales de la pobreza y de la desigualdad en Latinoamérica. *Revista de Victimología*, n. 7, pp. 47 ff.

48. Torrente, D. (2016). *Análisis de la seguridad privada*. Barcelona: Editorial UOC, pp. 13 ff.
49. The fanciful construction of these prejudiced characteristics does not prevent them—as we have already shown—from producing very real consequences in the social lives of the vulnerable. What exists in the social world is not confined to what is visible or measurable; in social phenomenology, existence is more closely tied to the *phenomenic actions* of individuals oriented toward a given direction.
50. Nascimento, A. do (1978). *O genocídio do negro brasileiro. Processo de um racismo mascarado*. Rio de Janeiro: Paz e Terra, pp. 41 ff.
51. Almeida, S. (2019). *Racismo estrutural*. São Paulo: Pólen Editorial, pp. 41 ff.
52. Souza, J. (2020). *A guerra contra o Brasil*. Rio de Janeiro: Estação Brasil, pp. 22 ff.
53. Pozuelo Pérez, L. (2013). *La política criminal mediática. Génesis, desarrollo y costes*. Madrid: Marcial Pons, pp. 16 ff.
54. Cervini Sánchez, R. (1994). Incidencia de las "mass media" en la expansión del control penal en Latinoamérica. *Revista Brasileira de Ciências Criminais*, n. 5, v. 2, pp. 47 ff.
55. Batista, V. M. (1997). Intolerância dez, ou a propaganda é a alma do negócio. *Discursos Sediciosos: Crime, Direito e Sociedade*, n. 4, v. 2, pp. 217 ff.
56. Wacquant, L. (1999). *Les prisons de la misère*. Paris: Raisons d'agir, pp. 9 ff.; Brandariz García, J. Á. (2019). *La economía política de la pena: una introducción*. Madrid: Iustel, pp. 83 ff.
57. Gauchet, M. (2016). Droite et gauche en redéfinition. *Le Débat*, n. 192, v. 5, pp. 35 ff.
58. Bobbio, N. (2014). *Destra e Sinistra. Ragioni e significati di una distinzione politica* (Edizione del ventennale con una introduzione di Massimo L. Salvadori e due commenti vent'anni dopo di Daniel Cohn-Bendit e di Matteo Renzi). Roma: Piccola Biblioteca Donzelli, pp. 147–148.
59. Bobbio, N. (2014). *Destra e Sinistra. Ragioni e significati di una distinzione politica* (Edizione del ventennale con una introduzione di Massimo L. Salvadori e due commenti vent'anni dopo di Daniel Cohn-Bendit e di Matteo Renzi). Roma: Piccola Biblioteca Donzelli, pp. 147–148.
60. Karam, M. L. (2021). *A esquerda punitiva: vinte e cinco anos depois*. São Paulo: Tirant lo Blanch.
61. Cano, I. & Santos, N. (2007). *Violência letal, renda e desigualdade no Brasil*. Rio de Janeiro: 7letras, pp. 9 ff.
62. Bettiol, G. (1948). *Il problema penale*. Palermo: Priulla, pp. 34 ff.
63. Benito Sánchez, D. (2020). *Evidencia empírica y populismo punitivo: el diseño de la política criminal*. Barcelona: Bosch Editor, pp. 27 ff.
64. Calvo García, M. (1994). *Los fundamentos del método jurídico: una revisión crítica*. Madrid: Editorial Tecnos, p. 282.
65. Morin, E. (1996). *Introduction à la pensée complexe*. Paris: ESF, pp. 23 ff.; Sousa Santos, B. (2002). *Introdução a uma ciência pós-moderna*. Porto: Edições Afrontamento, pp. 17 ff.
66. Maciver, R. M. & Page, C. H. (1958). *Sociología*. Madrid: Editorial Tecnos, pp. 15 ff.
67. Pozuelo Pérez, L. (2013). *La política criminal mediática. Génesis, desarrollo y costes*. Madrid: Marcial Pons, pp. 157 ff.
68. Supremo Tribunal Federal. (2015). *Arguição de Descumprimento de Preceito Fundamental n. 347 MC/DF*. Opinion by Justice Marco Aurélio. Full judgment, Plenary of the STF, pp. 1–210.

Bibliography

Alexy, R. (1993). *Teoría de los derechos fundamentales*. Centro de Estudios Constitucionales.

Almeida, S. (2019). *Racismo estrutural*. Pólen Editorial.

Aniyar de Castro, L. (1987). *Criminología de la liberación*. Editorial de la Universidad del Zulia.

Arroyo Zapatero, L. (1987). Fundamento y función del sistema penal: el programa penal de la Constitución. *Revista Jurídica de Castilla - La Mancha, 1*.

Bandeira de Mello, C. A. (2011). *O conteúdo jurídico do princípio da igualdade*. Malheiros Editores.

Batista, V. M. (1997). Intolerância dez, ou a propaganda é a alma do negócio. *Discursos Sediciosos: Crime, Direito e Sociedade, 2*(4).

Beccaria, C. (1964). *Dei delitti e delle pene*. Facsimile dell'edizione originale pubblicata anonima in livorno nel 1764 con le aggiunte delle successive edizioni e degli autografi registrate in margine e su carte allegate dal marchese giulio beccaria, figlio dell'Autore. Utet.

Bechara, A. E. L. S. (2015). As mortes sem pena no Brasil: A difícil convergência entre Direitos Humanos, política criminal e Segurança Pública. *Revista da Faculdade de Direito da Universidade de São Paulo, 110*.

Benito Sánchez, D. (2020). *Evidencia empírica y populismo punitivo: El diseño de la política criminal*. Bosch Editor.

Berdugo Gómez de la Torre, I. (2017). *La justicia transicional en Brasil. El caso de la guerrilla de Araguaia*. Ediciones Universidad de Salamanca.

Bettiol, G. (1948). *Il problema penale*. Priulla.

Blanco Lozano, C. (2007). *Tratado de política criminal. Tomo I: Fundamentos científicos y metodológicos de la lucha contra el delito*. Bosch Editor. pp. 155 ff; Sánchez-Ostiz, P. (2012). *Fundamentos de política criminal: un retorno a los principios*. Madrid: Marcial Pons, pp. 87 ff.

Bobbio, N. (2014). *Destra e sinistra. ragioni e significati di una distinzione politica (Edizione del ventennale con una introduzione di massimo l. salvadori e due commenti vent'anni dopo di Daniel Cohn-Bendit e di Matteo Renzi)*. Piccola Biblioteca Donzelli.

Bobbio, N. (2020). *Eguaglianza e libertà*. Einaudi.

Bobbio, N., Matteucci, N., & Pasquino, G. (1983). *Dizionario di politica*. UTET.

Bourdieu, P. (1993). *La misère du monde*. Éditions du Seuil.

Brandão, C. (2019). Poder e seletividade: Os processos de criminalização na América Latina e os seus impactos na crise do discurso penal. *Caderno de Relações Internacionais, 10*(18).

Brandariz García, J. Á. (2014). *El gobierno de la penalidad. La Complejidad de la política criminal contemporánea*. Editorial Dykinson.

Brandariz García, J. Á. (2019). *La economía política de la pena: Una introducción*. Iustel.

Bustos Ramírez, J., & Larrauri, E. (1993). *Victimología: Presente y futuro. Hacia Un sistema penal de alternativas*. PPU.

Calvo García, M. (1994). *Los fundamentos del método jurídico: Una revisión crítica*. Editorial Tecnos.

Cano, I., & Santos, N. (2007). *Violência letal, renda e desigualdade no brasil*. 7letras.

Cervini Sánchez, R. (1994). Incidencia de las "mass media" en la expansión del control penal en Latinoamérica. *Revista Brasileira de Ciências Criminais, 2*(5).

Dallari, D. A. (2016). *Elementos de teoria geral do estado*. Saraiva.

Del Mar Daza Bonachela, M. (2016). *Escuchar a las víctimas. Victimología, Derecho victimal y atención a las víctimas*. Tirant lo Blanch.

Demetrio Crespo, E. (2020). *El derecho penal del Estado de derecho entre el espíritu de nuestro tiempo y la Constitución*. Reus.

Dias Dos Santos, Í. (2017). Observatório da vida estudantil. Três itinerários de pesquisa: I. In G. G. D. Santos, L. Vasconcelos, & S. M. R. Sampaio (Eds.), *Observatório da vida estudantil. Dez anos de estudos sobre vida e cultura universitária* (pp. 271–279). Edufba.

Do Nascimento, A. (1978). *O genocídio do negro brasileiro. Processo de um racismo mascarado.* Paz e Terra.

Dworkin, R. (1989). *Los derechos en serio* (pp. 31 ff). Editorial Ariel.

Ferrajoli, L. (2019). *Manifesto per l'uguaglianza.* Laterza.

Feuerbach, P. J. A. (1800). *Revision der Grundsätze und Grundbegriffe des positiven peinlichen Rechts (Band 2).* Georg Friedrich Tasché.

Garland, D. (2011). *The culture of control. Crime and social order in contemporary society.* Oxford University Press.

Gauchet, M. (2016). Droite et gauche en redéfinition. *Le Débat, 5*(192).

Gil Villa, F. (2013). *Introducción a las teorías criminológicas. Por qué rompemos con la norma.* Tecnos.

Gomes Canotilho, J. J. (2003). *Direito constitucional e teoria da constituição.* Almedina.

Graef, B. (2023). Onde mora a impunidade? Porque o Brasil precisa de um Indicador Nacional de Esclarecimento de Homicídios. In *Instituto Sou da Paz.* São Paulo.

Instituto Brasileiro de Geografia e Estatística. (2019). *Síntese de indicadores sociais: Uma análise das condições de vida da sociedade brasileira contemporânea.* IBGE.

Karam, M. L. (2021). *A esquerda punitiva: Vinte e cinco anos depois.* Tirant lo Blanch.

Kramer, H., & Sprenger, J. (2004). *Malleus maleficarum: El martillo de las brujas. Para golpear a las brujas y sus herejías con poderosa maza.* Maxtor.

Lombroso, C. (1884). *L'uomo delinquente in rapporto all'antropologia, giurisprudenza ed alle discipline carcerarie. Delinquente nato e pazzo moral (terza edizione completamente rifatta con 17 tavole e 8 figure nel testo).* Fratelli Bocca.

Londoño Berrío, H. L. (2016). *Sistemas punitivos y derechos humanos: El caso de la Comuna 13 de Medellín - Colombia.* Ediciones Jurídicas Andrés Morales.

Machiavelli, N. (2019). *Il Principe.* Feltrinelli Editore.

Maciver, R. M., & Page, C. H. (1958). *Sociología.* Editorial Tecnos.

Mir Puig, S. (2011). *Bases constitucionales del derecho penal.* Iustel.

Moccia, S. (2002). Sul difficile rapporto tra principio di sussidiarietà, diritti fondamentali e politica criminali agli albori della postmodernità. In *Diritti dell'uomo e sistema penale* (Vol. I). Edizioni Scientifiche Italiane.

Moreira, A. (2019). *Racismo recreativo.* Pólen.

Morin, E. (1996). *Introduction à la pensée complexe.* ESF.

Morin, E. (2020). *Changeons de Voie: Les leçons du coronavirus (avec la colaboración de Sabah Abouessalam).* Éditions Denoël.

Nascimento, A. D. (1978). *O genocídio do negro brasileiro. Processo de um racismo mascarado.* Paz e Terra.

Neppi Modona, G., & Pelissero, M. (1997). La politica criminale durante il fascismo. In L. Violante (Ed.), *Storia d'Italia. Annali 12. La criminalità.* Einaudi.

Neves, M. (1994). *A constitucionalização simbólica.* Editora Acadêmica.

Neves, M. (2013). *Entre Hidra E Hércules: Princípios e regras constitucionais como diferença paradoxal do sistema jurídico.* Martins Fontes.

Oliveira Pires, T. R. (2017). Criminologia crítica e pacto narcísico: Por uma crítica criminológica apreensível em pretuguês. *Revista Brasileira de Ciências Criminais, 135*, 25.

Pepino, L. (2012). *Forti con i deboli.* Bur.

Piketty, T. (2014). *El capital en el siglo XXI.* Fondo de Cultura Económica.

Piketty, T. (2015). *La economía de las desigualdades: Cómo implementar una redistribución justa y eficaz de la riqueza.* Siglo Veintiuno Editores.

Pozuelo Pérez, L. (2013). *La política criminal mediática. Génesis, desarrollo y costes.* Marcial Pons.

Ruggiero, V. (2013). *I crimini dell'economia: Una lettura criminologica del pensiero economico.* Feltrinelli Editore.

Saad-Diniz, E., & Bessoni Boudoux Salgado, A. (2018). Violencia y victimización como costos sociales de la pobreza y de la desigualdad en Latinoamérica. *Revista de Victimología, 7.*

Sousa Santos, B. (2002). *Introdução a uma ciência pós-moderna*. Edições Afrontamento.
Sousa Santos, B. (2018). *Esquerdas do mundo, uni-vos*. Boitempo.
Souza, J. (2017). *A elite do atraso: Da escravidão à Lava Jato*. Leya.
Souza, J. (2018). *Subcidadania brasileira: Para entender o país além do jeitinho brasileiro*. Leya.
Souza, J. (2020). *A Guerra contra o Brasil*. Estação Brasil.
Souza, J., et al. (2018). *A ralé brasileira: Quem é e como vive*. Editora Contracorrente.
Spee, F. (2017). *Cautio Criminalis: Cautela Criminal*. Ediar.
Stiglitz, J. (2007). *Making Globalization Work*. Norton & Company.
Stiglitz, J. (2012). *El precio de la desigualdad: El 1 por ciento de la población tiene lo que el 99 por ciento necesita*. Taurus.
Stiglitz, J. (2018). *Globalization and Its Discontents Revisited: Anti-Globalization in the Era of Trump*. Norton & Company.
Supremo Tribunal Federal. (2015). *Arguição de Descumprimento de Preceito Fundamental, 347 MC/DF*. Opinion by Justice Marco Aurélio. Full Judgment, Plenary of the STF.
Tamarit Sumalla, J. M., Pereda, N., & Salinero, S. (2013). La victimización de las personas inmigrantes. In N. Pereda Beltran & J. M. Tamarit Sumalla (Eds.), *Victimología teórica y aplicada*. Huygens Editorial.
Tavares, J. (1997). A crescente legislação penal e os discursos de emergência. *Discursos Sediciosos: Crime, Direito E Sociedade*, *2*(4).
Terradillos Basoco, J. M. (2020). *Aporofobia y plutofilia: La deriva jánica de la política criminal contemporánea*. Bosch Editor.
Thomas, W. I., & Thomas, D. S. (1928). *The child in America: Behavior problems and programs*. Knopf.
Torrente, D. (2001). *Desviación y delito*. Alianza Editorial.
Torrente, D. (2016). *Análisis de la seguridad privada*. Editorial UOC.
Wacquant, L. (1999). *Les prisons de la misère*. Raisons d'agir.
Wacquant, L. (2007). *Parias urbains: Ghetto, banlieues, État*. La Découverte.
Wolfgang Sarlet, I. (2010). *A eficácia dos direitos fundamentais: Uma teoria geral dos direitos fundamentais na perspectiva constitucional*. Livraria do Advogado Editora.
Zaffaroni, R. (2010). *Crímenes de Masa*. Ediciones Madres de Plaza de Mayo.
Zaffaroni, R., & Dias Dos Santos, Í. (2020). *La nueva crítica criminológica. Criminología en tiempos de totalitarismo financiero*. Tirant lo Blanch.
Zúñiga Rodríguez, L. (2001). *Política criminal*. Colex.

Chapter 4
From Radical Analysis to Competent Criticism

4.1 Aporophobia and Penal Selectivity

In light of the foregoing, we maintain that *aporophobia* cannot serve as a critical-criminological concept of penal selectivity, as it proves to be a failed category, lacking heuristic elements capable of translating its analysis into an emancipatory critique. In other words, *aporophobia,* as a critique of punitive power, overlooks essential and sensitive elements necessary to grasp its latent structures.

This thesis applies to the current trend that continues to denounce the traditional selectivity historically constitutive of punitive power—or to that trend that merely intuits a transformation in this selectivity but fails to identify its origin or foundation, thereby lacking clarity on the basis of this new dynamic of penal selectivity.

The traditional model of selectivity in punitive power no longer exists in its original form. Due to the ongoing processes of *globalization,*[1] which simultaneously bring together and separate ethnolandscapes while intensifying sociopolitical idiosyncrasies, this selectivity—understood here as the original sin of punitive power—has undergone quantitative transformations (or, better said, *hyper-quantitative* ones), responsible for the spread of an unprecedentedly violent functioning of the penal system.

This selective dynamic has intensified over the last decades, as "Brazilian violence, like the entire country, operates in disproportionate terms; and the selectivity and arbitrariness of formal controls can be observed as the result of all this,"[2] even though its current peak of intensity is what we are now witnessing.

Thus, operating through the aforementioned *criminal policy of horror*—the criminal policy of the "other"—an exercise of uncontrolled punitive power is directed at the historically stereotyped, vulnerable groups in Brazilian society.

This dynamic acts as a powerful factor of class disorganization, as the excluded themselves strive to dissociate from this supposed caste by internalizing the same

Í. Dias Dos Santos, *Aporophobia and Punitive Power in Brazil*,
SpringerBriefs in Criminology,
https://doi.org/10.1007/978-3-032-01753-6_4

stereotypical values. Hence, the stereotype is also a fundamental issue to comprehend the current racial character of Brazilian penal selectivity.

Within this new configuration of *abysmal legal-penal selectivity*—where sensitive elements are largely responsible for its efficacy as a socially destabilizing and anti-democratic enterprise—*aporophobia*, when treated as a critical-criminological category, more than ever, reveals itself as limited in scope and, as such, sterile in any transformative sense regarding the criminological reality it seeks to confront.

4.2 The Dynamics of Abysmal Criminal Selectivity

The structural and structuring selectivity that has always marked the history of punitive power is no longer confined to the realm of social science but has become part of public knowledge. It is a *logisch-objektiv* fact, and denying it is not merely a theoretical or ideological matter—it is to marginalize an evident characteristic of the phenomenon under scrutiny. Law, when it denies a fact of reality, ceases to refer to the object it purports to address.[3]

In the case of the selectivity of punitive power, one may choose to justify or criticize it—both positions are ideological, but they refer to the same object. Denying it, on the other hand, while also ideological—at least by omission—results in a criminal law science indifferent to selectivity. More seriously still, it ends up referring to a nonexistent entity, a hallucinated abstraction: a nonselective punitive power. In such a case, whether it seeks to legitimize or criticize, it is no longer referring to punitive power as it actually exists in the world.

There comes a point in the development of civilization when what was once a scientific thesis enters the domain of general knowledge—such as the sphericity of the earth—which remains unaffected by the opinions of those who insist otherwise. In the same way, the selectivity of punitive power is no longer merely a hypothesis subject to verification; it has become a given, grounded in lived reality. It can no longer be elevated to the epistemic status of a thesis requiring methodological validation.

To regress from this understanding would be to legitimize the denial of a reality that, in itself, is indisputable to any researcher of the state who possesses intellectual honesty and scientific sensitivity. We live in such profoundly dehumanized times that, at times, reaffirming the obvious appears to be either revolutionary or extremist.

This does not mean, of course, that one should deny the need to reveal and investigate the particular forms that this undeniable selectivity assumes in specific contexts—especially when it reaches proportions of exceptional lack of control. The intensity and quality of this dynamic change over time, as dynamism is intrinsic to every human society and every form of power exercised within it.

In any society—and particularly in ours—it is not enough to recognize the structural character of punitive power as an abstract truth. It is essential to examine how its selective mechanisms are intensified, both quantitatively and qualitatively.

Only then can one take a critical and reflective stance on the phenomenon, with the aim of mitigating its harmful effects and elevating the standards of implementation of the principle of equality. This work is dedicated to precisely that inescapable academic endeavor.

4.3 A Criminological Critique of Our Ethnolandscape

The reference to Latin American critical criminology—and, subsequently, to the movement toward a criminology of the South—does not seek to demarcate a new field with its own independent methodology or epistemology. Quite the contrary, it points to the criminological movement that transferred critical postulates in criminology from other geographies to our Latin American margin, adapting and applying them to our own ethnolandscape without sacrificing the necessary conceptual rigor,[4] while discarding any form of exclusive scientific affectation in the face of our complex criminal issues.

It is a matter of reception: The critical paradigm of the second half of the twentieth century, taken up for sociopolitical adaptation in our context, revalued and reclaimed the discourse of human rights at the margins, promoting a criminological knowledge committed to the affirmation of human dignity and the liberation of our peoples, that is, a criminology that has sought to "allow us to do, in the face of the old criminology of repression, a criminology of liberation."[5]

In this way, Latin American criminology illuminated the distinctive features of punitive power in our region, forged through an intricate network of political, economic, and sociocultural dependence of our South on the North. It is a *criminological theory* that claims ownership in the sense that it does not merely reproduce what has been produced elsewhere for other realities dissonant from our own.

In this spirit, it proposed to overcome the model of etiological criminology—until then dominant—which rendered impossible any scientific knowledge of our criminal reality. That model, by design, prevented the formulation of any minimally emancipatory alternative for prevention, since "you cannot prevent what is not known, or what is known in a distorted, partialized, and disconnected way from the reality in which it arises,"[6] as seems to be the case with all uncritical importations of knowledge.

4.4 The Universal Contribution Is Only Valid If It Understands the Local Reality

While in the North there were full or intermediate welfare states, our Latin American states never attained that level of materialization of equality, having always oscillated between a "state of social discomfort" and an incipient welfare state. Taking this difference into account, Latin American critique sought to go beyond what was offered from realities marked by the consolidation and expansion of rights,[7] since, in our region, the struggle has always been for their initial conquest—except in sporadic episodes of expanded real citizenship, generally met with violent containment.[8]

This political-economic framework entails a marked intensification of punitive violence in our South, amplifying its selectivity,[9] which traps increasing numbers of socioeconomically vulnerable individuals. Moreover, everything seems to indicate that this operates as a way to "reinforce the antagonisms generated by stratification and increase the degree of irritation in societies already unsettled by a broader framework of notorious social injustice,"[10] thus widening the well-known gap between the manifest and latent functions of punitive power.[11]

Given that punitive power in our region is notoriously more selective—due to the characteristics of socioeconomic vulnerability—we are compelled to account for how this vulnerability impacts the criminal question, not merely to understand it but to extend this understanding into the legal field. For this, "in our margin, we need knowledge that enables us to explain what our penal systems are, how they operate, what effects they produce, why and how those effects are concealed, what connection they maintain with broader forms of social control and power, what alternatives exist to this reality, and how they might be implemented,"[12] that is, *a criminology from the margin, about the margin, and for the Latin American margin.*

In this sense, it is clear that we cannot ignore the universal traits of punitive power, but what must be imposed is the rejection of what is not inherent to our reality—that is, its accidental characteristics. This does not entail advocating for a fragmentation of criminology, as if to claim a self-contained criminology for each locale, which would dissolve into the ether of rhetorical emptiness. It is clear that what is scientifically verified in Europe—under the same methodological premises—is also valid in America, insofar as it concerns characteristics inherent to any exercise of punitive power: The instrument remains the same, but the object of study differs. In our case, it is about analyzing punitive power in an underdeveloped context and in the absence of a social state.[13]

It may also occur that the instrument proves insufficient and, in our case, that imported critique fails to capture essential heuristic elements for understanding another reality. This would necessitate the construction of a convergent theoretical framework—an improvement of our microscope—because social reality is hypercomplex and cannot be singular. Consequently, adequate responses cannot be singular either. In such a case, *the refinement of our instrument would constitute a new contribution to criminology, as it would render visible phenomena not captured by the instruments of the North.*

It is worth recalling that this perspective entered our region cautiously but firmly. Its caution was due to the political climate that devastated the continent at the time of the arrival of criminological critique, plagued by authoritarian regimes—the so-called "national security dictatorships"—in which critical criminological knowledge could not be disseminated without being delegitimized from various quarters, and its thinkers and researchers were even subjected to repression. For this reason, this criminology first took root in the Latin American countries least affected by such dictatorships—though not entirely free from punitive violence—emerging as an alternative to traditional etiological or positivist criminology.[14]

In academic circles—the principal site of ideological reproduction—criticisms ranged from healthy debate over the *scientific character*[15] and the very existence of a *Latin American criminology*[16] to the *political stigmatization* of its proponents, which persists to some extent today as a tactical tool of power to achieve the strategic goal of destabilization. Despite these difficulties, that goal was not achieved, as evidenced by the many scientific events, meetings, debates, and academic collaborations that unfolded during the consolidation of Latin American criminology and continue to this day, attesting to the enduring relevance of critical criminology in the region.[17]

The study of criminology as critical knowledge began in an autodidactic manner, as public universities—despite being emancipatory institutions with a social responsibility,[18] whose fundamental purpose includes the critical and reflective formation of technically, artistically, and humanistically competent citizens (note well: cumulatively),[19] paradoxically relegated criminological knowledge, reducing it to brief, merely theoretical introductions, even when it is evident that it is an empirical and interdisciplinary field of knowledge.

It is clear that this marginalization constituted a formidable contribution to the misunderstanding of our legal-penal particularities,[20] which demand depth, connections, and all manner of interrelations as a *conditio sine qua non* for comprehending our complex phenomena.

However, little by little, this critical perspective gained substance and made its way into the pantheons of university life—especially after the democratic transitions—being incorporated into the political and social debates of our region, producing changes in the discourse around our particular criminal issue. These transformations even reached some of the most refined cultivators of legal-penal dogmatics in the South, who, each in their own way, began to give shape to a *penal-dogmatic realism* in the region.[21]

Thus, a criminological thought epistemologically committed to our margin gradually took shape across the region, albeit with varying degrees of intensity. This thought sought not only to *see*, but to *make others see*, the notion that "without seeking an interpretation of the world from our place—which, in turn, transforms the interpretation of our place—we will make no valid contribution to the knowledge of the world,"[22] much less to the knowledge of our place.

4.5 From Trickle Genocide to Flood Genocide

As previously noted, punitive power is frequently placed at the service of power itself,[23] which is why it reflects, in its mutations, the changes occurring in the latter.[24] In this respect, we cannot disregard the transformations brought about by the *hypercomplexity* of contemporary societies, by the varied effects of *globalization*—which selectively and strategically bring closer or distance *ethnolandscapes* according to hegemonic interests[25]—by the super-technological advances of recent decades and their consequences for regional and global power, as well as by new forms of dependency, which further widen the North–South divide.

However, these changes in the symbolic and factual apparatuses of punitive power, while introducing new methods and intensifying existing ones in the direction of characteristic selectivity, result predominantly in quantitative—or rather, *superquantitative*—rather than strictly qualitative changes. This does not imply, of course, that punitive power does not experience operational refinements over time; yet, despite these, it never ceases to be a structural phenomenon.[26]

In any case, the critical theoretical framework developed in those early years remains fully valid and alive—especially in terms of highlighting transversal features of punitive power: the manifest deterioration of prison conditions, the impunity of socioeconomic crimes, the inversely proportional relationship between financial power and punitive vulnerability, the deceptive allure of simplistic punitive solutions,[27] the criminalizing selection of stereotyped and vulnerable individuals from the lowest socioeconomic strata or marginalized ethnic, sexual, and cultural groups, and so on.[28]

The critique of the *violent operability* of punitive power has reached such a degree of *normalization*—so habitual that it no longer draws attention—that even executions without trial, producing countless deaths, generate no local or international alarm. This silence is largely due to the normalizing contribution of hegemonic media (whether monopolistic, oligopolistic, or simply dominant) and the incorporation of this dynamic by its agents[29] in a kind of *rehearsed choreography of lethality*.

To this must be added the lethal conflict fostered and tolerated by institutional structures of punitive power, which pits the most vulnerable against one another—those who belong to the same social sectors—with the clear objective of deepening internal conflict and unleashing daily lethal violence. The result is what could be described as a real *trickle genocide*,[30] driven by the unrestrained deployment of punitive power. The underlying logic of this process is the fragmentation of resistance: Resistance to domination is not built by the dominated.

These lethal dynamics have dramatically intensified in the region, where death tolls increasingly resemble those of great genocidal historical conflicts. Such deaths are no longer merely announced and normalized—they are often celebrated or incited through media narratives constructed from *biased imagery*.[31]

Daily homicides among the vulnerable no longer come drop by drop; it is as if the floodgates of horror have been opened (*flood genocide*), producing torrents of death. The tone now goes beyond naturalization to a sort of incitement to elimination—of a human being reified by the "criminal policy of the other," upon whom repression is concentrated. No one wishes to identify with this subject, cast as the generator of criminality, in a return to Lombrosian determinism.

Since the 1990s, denunciations have been made regarding the lethality practiced by so-called death squads against children. At the time, it was described as follows: "There is a fragmented and growing process of extermination of minor offenders or alleged offenders, a policy that has the support or connivance of broad social segments, frightened by the insecurity of large urban centers. It especially counts on the participation, support, or connivance of the police."[32]

The favored target of this lethal victimization is always minors. The alleged increase in juvenile delinquency is a persistent refrain of the criminalizing media discourse. Just as positivists affirmed a century ago, so too do today's opinion *(de) formers* in regional media monopolies: Juvenile delinquency has never ceased to increase. Nearly a century ago, one could read: "In almost all civilized countries, where criminal statistics can be considered reliable, a lamentable trend has been observed in recent years: the criminality of childhood and adolescence is on the rise, revealing, day by day, increasingly precocious antisocial impulses."[33]

It is evident, however, that the statistics referenced at the time were those of criminalization, not the actual frequency of crime. And, if this increase were true for over a century, one would have to conclude that today's entire childhood and adolescent population consists of precocious delinquents.

The truth is that we are immersed in a historically unprecedented process of lethal innocuousness executed by punitive power. It is not only the well-known structural penal selectivity—to which punitive power has always been historically linked[34]—but also, in our time, a global power that has restructured its strategic lines, generating a kind of *hyperselectivity aimed at the most vulnerable*. And not only them, for punitive power also seeks scapegoats or the neutralization of other social groups that might disturb or obstruct hegemonic interests.

4.6 What is Abysmal Penal Selectivity?

The current context of deepening in the selectivity of punitive power leads us to consider Boaventura de Sousa Santos's notion of *abysmal thinking*, a generator of inequalities, especially as it reveals that, in our region, some individuals are not merely excluded but pushed far beyond the threshold of exclusion—rendered completely invisible in terms of their own human condition,[35] as well as from the cultural perspective and the knowledge they produce as a society.[36]

In Latin America, historically a gathering point for the world's excluded, we may say that we are facing a form of *abysmal legal-criminal selectivity* in the exercise of punitive power.

This selectivity is *abysmal* because it intensifies, to historically unprecedented levels, the characteristic inequalities of Latin America—constructing and labeling the *abysmally excluded* for secondary criminalization, and rapidly implementing a state policy that creates excluded *untermenschen* (subhumans, nonpersons, the invisibilized). This policy manifests as a catastrophic criminal policy targeting the weakest among the weak, where all indications suggest that institutional centrality has shifted decisively toward criminal matters.

This criminogenic policy—revealed by the quantitative transformations in penal selectivity—causes a genuine deterioration of the Rule of Law, as it compromises even the minimum level of social harmony.[37] It fosters the proliferation of a *pluralization of uncontrolled punitive systems*,[38] even beyond the known parallel or subterranean systems, in line with the warnings of Latin American critical criminology from previous decades.[39]

The lethal violence alone, officially recorded in Latin America (and which reflects only part of the phenomenon), is already telling of the abyssal trend of selective violence and the turning point the region has reached. This is a criminal policy successful only in terms of body count—one that has escalated exponentially in recent decades.[40]

Beyond this lethality—whether perpetrated by police forces or in the form of other crimes such as torture[41]—the region's penitentiary systems also reflect this new *abysmal penal selectivity* through mass incarceration, adopted as a state policy[42] regardless of the ideological orientation of the sitting government.[43]

Brazil represents a paradigmatic case in the region, due to both the scale of its mass incarceration and its strategic geopolitical relevance within Latin America. With one of the largest prison populations in the world, approximately 40% of people deprived of liberty in the country are in pretrial detention (imprisoned without conviction), which reflects a concerning trivialization of this precautionary measure.[44]

Of this figure, only about 11% corresponds to people accused of homicide—indicating a clear mismatch between the country's homicide rate and its high incarceration rate. Moreover, the prison system operates with a deficit exceeding 50%,[45] meaning that a significant number of arrest warrants remain unexecuted due to a lack of space, while those that are enforced largely follow the discretionary criteria of punitive agencies.[46]

The most frequently applied criminal offense used to incarcerate individuals in Brazil—as in most countries in the region—is drug trafficking, accounting for around 30% of the prison population. These cases usually involve small-scale users, selected through stereotyping, or, at most, minor distributors.

Another major driver of mass incarceration across the region is crimes against property, particularly theft and robbery—traditionally regarded as poverty-related offenses.[47] This trend is supported by the socioeconomic profiles of the incarcerated: mostly young people, members of racial and ethnic minorities, and individuals without access to education—in societies where such factors are the primary indicators of social vulnerability. This reality underscores the prevalence of *abysmal legal-criminal selectivity* in the region.

4.7 The Power Framework That Conditions the Abyssal Legal-Criminal Selectivity

Having highlighted some of the exacerbated structural characteristics of the exercise of punitive power in the Latin American reality—characteristics that must be critically investigated—it becomes necessary to explore the reasons behind the *shift in its objectives*. The classic selective tools of punitive power have not disappeared; rather, they have been intensified and redirected *toward new functions*. This redirection demands a critical analysis anchored in a thorough revision of the critiques we have produced thus far, with the aim of expanding their theoretical, methodological, and epistemological boundaries.[48]

Such critical renewal is imperative today, as it becomes evident that previous critiques—many of which still persist—were aimed at a punitive power embedded in a power framework that has either changed or is in the process of changing. That earlier framework was characteristic of peripheral and productive capitalism, which bears little resemblance to the current scenario marked by the dismantling of the welfare state—experienced to varying degrees—and its associated consumer societies, also unevenly realized.[49]

In Latin America, although we never fully attained a welfare state, we did experience a form of peripheral capitalism. Today, however, we are witnessing its accelerated dismantling,[50] giving way to the dystopia of unlimited wealth concentration. This generates a *chronic* condition of underdevelopment, with the rapid deterioration of living standards among large segments of the population,[51] fostering violent conflict through chaotic penal apparatuses (the repressive face of the state) and the perpetuation of social exclusion (the absent social face of the state).

This geopolitical conditioning appears as an *advanced phase of colonialism*—or *late-colonialism*—that distorts democracies and appropriates politics, transferring *real political power* from the states to the CEOs of transnational corporations. The states of the Global South are placed under the command of local proconsuls serving late-colonial interests, undermining domestic productive capital, stigmatizing political actors deemed dysfunctional, promoting *anti-politics*, and elevating outsider politicians destined to serve as these proconsuls.[52] Among the main instruments of this power are concentrated media and the manipulation of punitive power.[53]

The model of society taking shape in this planetary power turn—reflected in our region—completely alters the cooperation and conflict dynamics typical of productive capitalism, the principal object of earlier criminological critique. It replaces the classic dialectic of *exploiter and exploited* with a new non-dialectical binary: *included and excluded*. This is a hallmark of financial capitalism, whose mechanisms have become hypertrophied to dominate the productive sector.[54] On the microsocial level, it seeks to provoke a cultural shift by disseminating a *false meritocratic dialectic of winners and losers*.

Thus, the new sociopolitical dynamic bears no resemblance to the so-called dual society—or *society of thirds*—once envisioned (though often unrealized) by productive peripheral capitalism.[55] That model, ideologically structured around *two-thirds* of the population enjoying the benefits of consumer society while one-third remained circumstantially excluded, has been progressively replaced. Today, what used to be a dual society—where "two-thirds of the population lived better than ever"[56]—has given way to an ideological model of a *unidirectional society* striving for a structurally excluded majority.

This totalitarian project of ever-increasing and incessant wealth concentration appears to require the imposition of a social model in which a minority of the included (30%) coexists with a *structurally* excluded majority (70%)—the so-called 30/70 model.[57]

Given the high degree of sociospatial upheaval inevitably caused by endemic exclusion, this program requires from the punitive power an increasingly criminalizing selection of all those who may represent nuisances to its interests—especially the excluded themselves, though not exclusively—by promoting local violence through mass incarceration, the distribution and encouragement of weapon possession, the militarization of policing, and other measures that operate as a kind of *immunodeficiency virus, weakening underdeveloped states*. In this vicious cycle, popular sectors—seduced by a falsified autocratic media discourse and struck by victimization—demand even more violence, which is eventually turned against them through the selection of the stereotyped or the containment of their demands.[58]

Moreover, this perverse management is not limited to the traditionally stigmatized subjects—such as the proletariat or lumpenproletariat of old Marxist analyses, which inspired much of last century's radical criminology. Although they continue to be labeled, new subaltern classes are now invented through media monopolies (which themselves are transnational corporations),[59] giving life to stereotypes of subhuman enemies who condense the worst social prejudices, seducing even the most disadvantaged into distancing themselves from such figures and considering themselves superior.[60] These media fictions are reinforced through the secondary selection of the excluded and a permanent discourse of emergencies.[61]

In the end, this global turn signals an overwhelming tendency toward financial totalitarianism on a planetary scale.[62] It is totalitarian, first, because of its scope—it includes even the host countries of transnational corporations, albeit with nuances.[63] Its totalitarian nature also lies in its concealment under a singular ideology that proclaims itself *neoliberal* and reduces all knowledge—especially social knowledge—to market logic (market reductionism).[64] Its deviant anthropology invents a *homo economicus* naturally destined for the indefinite accumulation of wealth. Its totalizing, reductionist, and obscurantist drive leads it to exclude, stigmatize, and even repress all critical reflection.[65]

This aversion to criticism arises because it lifts the reductionist veil and brings attention to social and especially economic facts, thus revealing the real aims of the current regional socioeconomic model: the perpetuation of exclusion. It also reveals the *pan-punitivist* nature of its criminal policy, which shapes the so-called *common crime* of our region—crime that is not only functional to the exclusionary design but also to the weakening of states and democracies, thereby facilitating the continuation of late colonization.[66]

4.8 The Necessary Renewal of Criminological Critique in the South and the North

What we have tried to do in this brief reflection is to highlight the central axes of the suicidal social strategy undertaken by our states, which ultimately seem destined to destroy any viable project of a democratic and plural society. From this arises the methodological and intellectual imperative to renew the criminological critique of the South so that it may respond with creativity and innovation to the increasing intensity of the selective features of punitive power. In other words, so that it may see, *make seen*, and *contain* the current abyssal legal-criminal selectivity.

We propose this with the caveat that such a critique aims to look at the South from the South, but without presuming that there exists an *old* and a *new* critique in which the latter supersedes the former in a hierarchical fashion. Rather, the intention is to continue renewing the critical path of criminology in our region,[67] attentive to the fact that its object of study—our societies—has changed substantially. Not in vain have four long decades passed through our territories and through the structures of planetary power.

Nor can we ignore what we previously pointed out regarding the cost in human lives, which compels us to incorporate, as an object of analysis, the figures of ongoing state genocide—thus giving entry to a phenomenon that, at one point, was incorporated into the field of critical criminology due to its extreme gravity.[68]

We also do not intend to overlook the fact that the South we refer to is not geographical, but social and political;[69] that is, it does not seek to construct a radical territorial separation in the traditional sense of demarcated lines. We are fully aware that this is a *geographical space* that encompasses not only materiality but also the human perspective that animates it.[70] Put differently, one could say that there is *a South that inhabits the North and a North that cohabits in the South*—albeit in different proportions and intensities.

This means that the old North–South paradigm has been redefined—though not abolished—as the inequalities produced by the monopolistic distribution of global power, even at the technological level, remain largely concentrated in one part of the planet, despite being more dispersed today. This shift renders the traditional *center-periphery* division increasingly asymmetrical, as poverty and inequality also grow within the northern countries. In this regard, "there has also been an accentuation of uneven development, this time not only between North and South, but between the dynamic segments and territories of societies and those at risk of becoming irrelevant from the point of view of the system's logic,"[71] which is nothing but the logic of exclusion.

It can thus be clearly verified that the *North–South* division now presents new nuances, as evidenced by the deterioration of living standards in certain areas of the global North and by specific zones in the South where development resembles that of central countries. Nonetheless, the general tone of the current economic model—governed by supranational agencies based in central countries—remains unchanged, marked by the unilateral imposition of their interests on those below. Likewise, the reprehensible inequality and poverty in the developed world cannot be compared to the structural devastation experienced in the countries of the southern hemisphere, beginning with technological inequality, since "the differential opportunity in access to the power of technology for people, countries, and regions is a critical source of inequality in our society,"[72] whose consequences are disproportionately borne by the peoples of the South—even if, in their own way, some areas of the North also suffer from them.

As a result of this redefinition of the North–South dynamic, our proposal does not entail a radical methodological rupture with northern criminology. In this sense, the contradiction between a devotional belief in the general-preventive function of penalties (the harsher, the better) and the unlimited growth of technological control and surveillance—symptomatic of the decline of the welfare state in both hemispheres—is not entirely foreign to our South.[73] On the other hand, not only is *governance through fear/crime*—a phenomenon that threatens democracy by placing victimhood at the center of political discourse[74]—common to the North and South, but it is even more evident in our region, where the increasing precariousness of the productive capitalist model as a correlate of *punitivism* is particularly pronounced.[75]

4.9 The Criminology of Blindness

Although we are aware that the renewal of the critical path must be constant—and that the elements to be incorporated into this process vary according to time and space—there are, nonetheless, certain components that are unavoidable due to their power to generate criminalizing selection and the central role they play in the *current advanced phase of punitive selectivity*.

For this reason, the critical perspective of a criminology that seeks to analyze abyssal legal-criminal selectivity in the South cannot overlook the ethnic or racist component—often rendered invisible or minimized—despite its persistent relevance in our region, particularly in those countries that bear the deep scars of the transatlantic slave trade. Ignoring this would be akin to promoting, in our context, a form of *criminology of blindness*—one that, through totalizing or myopic concepts, prevents us from perceiving the actual causes of today's abyssal selectivity of punitive power.

Although criminology in our region has yet to fully integrate the ethnic or racist dimension as a central element nourishing punitive selectivity—and although it has not carefully examined the role played by selective stereotypes in this *advanced phase of criminal law selectivity*—it nonetheless offers us the tools we need to do so.

In sum, the entire tradition of critical criminological thinking equips us with essential theoretical, methodological, and epistemological instruments to confront—without circumlocution—the new challenges posed by our criminal issue in times of abyssal penal selectivity, an issue that is, at its core, a question of power and that, as such, always interweaves the universal with the local. For *the microphysics of punitive power* invariably responds to *the macrophysics of global power*—whose nature appears to be shifting in its content, methods, and objectives. To disregard this link would be to misplace our gaze on a peripheral dimension of the phenomenon while overlooking its very core.

4.10 What Are the Theoretical-Methodological Bases for the Criticism of Punitive Power?

A sensitive, critical formation is the indispensable condition for the task of seeing and making visible the empirical reality that surrounds punitive power on our margins. It provides the necessary heuristic elements so that the gaze may apprehend, in an appropriate and realistic way, the phenomena that intrinsically and extrinsically permeate our punitive power.

This critical and emancipatory formation cannot be achieved by traditional paths of linear or purely dogmatic knowledge, in which disciplines close in on themselves. Given the complexity acquired by phenomena of power—such as the punitive—no field or discipline, in isolation, holds the capacity to unveil its operations, let alone propose new paths.

This transformative formation, which enables subjects to position themselves critically and reflectively in relation to the penal and criminological question, must be accompanied by an open and *honest intellectual* posture. This means acknowledging that, in addressing each theme within our field, we adopt the stance of *participant observers*: We are, inevitably, politically, and ideologically contributing either to the consolidation or to the questioning of the penal condition.

In this sense, by clearing the way—without false asepsis or idealized scientificity—we open the possibility for a *prudent scientificity*, one whose guiding thread is the social responsibility inherent in all scientific practice committed to the postulates of the common good, or what we might also call the social and democratic Rule of Law.

This theoretical-methodological posture, nurtured by interdisciplinarity, proves to be an indispensable instrument for avoiding all forms of totalizing investigative myopia that obscure the complexity of legal-penal and criminological phenomena.

Aporophobia, when approached as a critical-criminological concept, seems to suffer precisely from a lack of interdisciplinarity in its analysis of the current abyssal legal-penal selectivity. One gets the impression that such analysis proceeds solely from legal-penal—specifically dogmatic—knowledge in its attempt to critique the exercise of punitive power.

However, as we will clarify later, beyond being methodologically inadequate, this stance ultimately contributes to the invisibilization and misunderstanding of the real causes that feed this abyssal selectivity. And as it is well said: "You cannot prevent what you do not know, or what you know in a distorted, partial, and disconnected way from the reality in which it originates."[76]

Thus, the theoretical and methodological foundation for the analysis of our punitive power must be one of realistic and empirically informed critique, capable of unveiling the real functioning of punitive power in its localized expressions; that is, "a knowledge that explains what our penal systems are, how they operate, what effects they produce, why and how these effects are hidden from us, what relationship they maintain with other mechanisms of social control and power, what alternatives exist to this reality, and how they can be implemented."[77]

Nevertheless, not even this marginal critical stance—in the sense of being produced in and for our Latin American margin—is sufficient by itself to apprehend the abyssal legal-criminal selectivity of punitive power in Brazil.

What is required is the renewal of this critical path through an interdisciplinary effort, allowing a new criminological critique to emerge—one that incorporates *local epistemologies*[78] as a force of renewal for the emancipatory critique developed in the last century. This theoretical stance is urgent, for with the change in the world power framework, the object once analyzed by that critique—traditional penal selectivity—has been transformed into abyssal legal-criminal selectivity. In other words, it now refers to an object that no longer exists as such.[79]

We are not, of course, advocating for the absolute negation of past criminological critique. Rather, we affirm the necessity of its renewal—wherever it may be required—so that it remains adequate for the analysis and critique of current punitive power.

It is from these theoretical-methodological foundations that any analysis or critique of our punitive power must begin. They are adequate to perceive—and to help others perceive—how it operates in both its real and symbolic facets, surfacing its generative and fostering elements, and clearly distinguishing the central from the accessory, so as to open the path to action.

4.11 Legal-Criminal Delegitimization and Aporophobia

The delegitimization of our punitive systems—understood either from the "irrationality of our current and operating penal systems"[80] or through the realization of the perennial impossibility of legitimizing any and all penal systems[81]—leads us toward the path of containing punitive power through the restrained use of criminal law as a supposed instrument of protection.

This delegitimization has a diffuse origin, for practically all criminological and sociological theories—including the classical ones—have been decisive in shedding light on the manifest and latent functions of punitive power, which ultimately contributed to its delegitimization.

In this sense, these theoretical perspectives have thus ended up revealing, clearly and with evidence, the falsity of the doctrinal assumptions that support legal-criminal knowledge, generating a kind of general panic among scholars in our field and an urgent need for reinvention.

Such was the case with the principle of culpability, questioned by the theory of criminal subcultures; the principle of good and evil, shaken by the theory of anomie; or the labeling theory, which dismantled the idea of prevention and, in its German version, even denied the very idea of equality.[82]

This paradigm deepened the distrust in both the discourse and practice of criminal law, opening space for the construction of a delegitimizing critique, in which legitimacy could only be claimed through marginal criminological realism, ultimately converging on a criminal law of containment. That is, "the alternative paradigm (paradigm of the social reaction) has put in the foreground, in the study of deviation and criminality, the mechanisms of definition and labeling, institutional and informal, and, consequently, the process of primary criminalization (formation of the criminal law) and secondary criminalization (application of the criminal law)."[83]

To this, we must add the delegitimizing critique of penal abolitionism, with its transformative potential. No other theoretical perspective has achieved such a universal critical transcendence of criminal law as the abolitionist movement—despite its internal nuances, including ideological and practical ones.[84]

The delegitimization proposed by abolitionism was perhaps the final major stronghold in the critical assault on criminal law, for its devastating analysis could not be evaded. Yet, the responses it received were mostly short-sighted: accusations of *utopianism*, defensive reactions, and refusals to recognize the importance of utopia in the transformation of reality.

Thus, a considerable portion of legal thought has ignored—and continues to ignore—the immense transformative power of abolitionist critique. Those who, on the contrary, perceive its force and attempt to respond by using delegitimization as a basis to legitimize criminal-legal knowledge through criticism deserve mention.

Given all the critique produced to date, it becomes clear that the path of delegitimization is the most appropriate for confronting the unrestrained punitive power in our region, especially in Brazil, where such lack of restraint has reached historically unprecedented levels. Any attempt at criticizing punitive power that ignores this basic premise cannot be understood as critique at all; it is, in truth, legitimizing punitive power—whether by action or by omission.

In this context, the construction of aporophobia as a critical criminological concept reveals an insurmountable methodological flaw: the belief in criminal law as an adequate instrument for overcoming the so-called aversion to the poor by seeking to construct normative instruments supposedly capable of protecting the targets of aporophobia.

Such a position, besides displaying a total idealization of the penal response—or even a *symbolic criminal law*[85]—completely disregards the historical experience of criminology, which has persistently shown that, in the rare instances where criminal law is said to provide protection—considering that criminal law protects something—it does so always selectively.

Therefore, when we consider aporophobia as a philosophical concept, we perceive that the proposal begins with the legitimization of criminal law as an appropriate tool for confronting a social problem—precisely the opposite path to that suggested by Franz von Liszt, who warned that "the best criminal policy is a good social policy."

Likewise, when we focus on aporophobia as a critical criminological concept—the object of this critical reflection—we realize that such a proposal, even if unconsciously, legitimizes criminal law (always selective) as an adequate means to combat aporophobic selectivity: a notion that is nothing short of absurd from a criminological perspective.

This stance neglects—either through negligence or subservience—the fact that "the subordinate classes are, in truth, negatively selected by the mechanisms of criminalization,"[86] and that criminal law, most often, serves as the very instrument of this selective criminalization. Therefore, its use must be strictly limited to the indispensable; criminal law is not a suitable tool for implementing social policy—let alone for containing the abyssal selectivity of punitive power.

4.12 The Very New Punitive Left of Criminal Aggravations

In a movement of idolatry of criminal law—in which even the critique of its selectivity falls into the simplistic trap of using it as a supposed instrument of social protection—the old belief in penal response as a means to contain violence re-emerges, disregarding the violent potential of punitive power against the vulnerable.

Thus arises a certain punitive left of aporophobia, aligned with the traditional old punitive left, where, "detached from a serious analysis of reality and accompanying the exacerbation of the punitive desire, which follows the immediate ideal of 'living in peace', even those sectors of the left do not find strange this desire for peace that even admits war."[87]

These are well-intentioned academic representatives of criminal law who, with an idealistic and dogmatic formation, seem unaware that by opening the doors to the formal penal response, a multitude of informal windows of violence and uncontrollable lethality are also opened—always, in Brazil, with a determined direction and skin color. In other words, "they do not realize that the general climate of exacerbation of the punitive desire, which counts on their decided support, is the great encourager of the violence of informal repression, directed against those who correspond to the image of criminals. They do not realize that the appeal to authority and order and the expansion of the punitive power of the state—the result of the demand for greater repression of crime—implies an increasing inhumanity in the fight against crime, favoring the deepening and cruelty of informal repression, whether through the illegal action of police officers, through the action of extermination groups, or through lynchings."[88]

This methodological mistake—and, as such, political-ideological—mortally wounds the transformative potential that has always characterized critical and informed academic knowledge. The fundamental task of those committed to containing the violence of punitive power is always its *containment in view of transformation*, because "this transformative path cannot be treated with the reproduction of the exclusionary mechanisms characteristic of the societies that one wants to transform. There is no way to achieve more generous and solidary societies using the same methods that one wants to overcome."[89]

This is not merely a discursive issue; it does not remain confined to the theoretical field and, therefore, cannot be remedied by dogmatic-penal strategies. One cannot overlook that appealing to the institute of penal aggravations as a theoretical device to avoid being labeled a punitivist does not possess, in itself, the capacity to alter the formal and informal selective force of punitive power in the real world.

In this light, the current trend of invoking penal aggravations to typify aporophobia as a crime is, to some extent, a *labeling fraud*. Even if this dogmatic strategy does not establish a specific criminal type, its criminological repercussions are the same: It opens a new selective field for punitive power.

This is precisely the trajectory embraced by those who defend aporophobia as a critical criminological concept. Virtually all of them arrive—unsurprisingly—at a penal response as a supposed solution to restrain aversion to the poor, seen as the generative cause of criminal aggressions. It could hardly be otherwise: The premise itself is flawed, rooted in an almost theological belief in criminal law; the stance is entrenched in dogmatic-penal knowledge; the functions of criminal law are legitimized without empirical basis; and the absence of interdisciplinary perspectives precludes the crossing of the river of single answers to complex problems.

All of this ultimately legitimizes not only punitive power in a theoretical and abstract sense but, more crucially, legitimizes what it claims to denounce: the inequality that characterizes punitive power and materializes through its executive agencies.

To believe that the executive agencies of punitive power—those responsible for abyssal selectivity—will suddenly protect their historically targeted audience (the vulnerable, the pariahs) through a penal aggravation, or that the operators of this same punitive system will abruptly cease to follow their stereotyped archetypes of the criminalized subject, is not only criminologically disconcerting but also incompatible with the manifest functions exercised by punitive power.

To place faith in penal aggravations as if they might acquire a resolutive or even preventive function in this matter is akin to imagining that someone intending to commit an aporophobic act would first consult the criminal code to assess the plausibility of their action—evaluating whether the penalty or its absence makes it worthwhile.

4.13 The Criminalization of Aporophobia

Following the Spanish movement toward the criminalization of aporophobia—based on its framing as a critical-criminological concept and advocating the creation of sentence aggravations, as discussed in the previous section—a similar, manifestly imported proposal has emerged in the Brazilian National Congress.

This proposal is grounded in the same rationale as its Spanish counterpart, which argues, in summary, for the inclusion of aporophobia as an aggravating factor within existing offenses in the Spanish Penal Code of 1995. The goal is to promote equality through a manifestly unequal instrument: "[. . .] there is a lack of an adequate and proportionate penal response (in addition to being materially fairer) to cases of crime committed for aporophobic reasons, as legal operators are not being provided with adequate tools for this purpose from the Penal Code. [. . .] The existence of a criminal law basis is grounded on a greater deserving and need for punishment in cases of crime committed for aporophobic reasons. The question that is added is a proposal of *lege ferenda* that allows the inclusion of these motivations among the catalog of conditions in the current art. 22.4º CP, which increases a penalty that is more deserved, as the value of equality is also violated."[90]

The Brazilian Bill in question exhibits the tone of both legislative and doctrinal production typically found in the country: an uncritical and automatic importation of theoretical and legislative precepts from foreign criminological realities, without the prior critical analysis necessary to evaluate their compatibility and adequacy.

The proposal transposes the Spanish criminological context to the Brazilian reality as if they were equivalent, relying, at most, on localized data from the homeless population in São Paulo to demonstrate that the violence they suffer stems from their condition of poverty, while disregarding the full range of stereotypical elements involved.

Toward the end of the project, the belief in criminal law as a mechanism to protect the vulnerable becomes explicit. The draft states that the proposed law "will protect people living on the streets from violence" and adds that, given the current economic crisis, social inequality in Brazil will likely deepen—hence the need for such a legislative initiative. Particular attention should be paid to the following passage: "In the face of not very optimistic prospects due to the recent economic crises, as well as the one we are about to enter due to the state of public calamity as a result of the COVID-19 pandemic, the trend, unfortunately, is for the poor population to increase. Therefore, these are the ones who suffer more and more each day from the violence that this Bill intends to protect."[91]

The attempt to employ the well-known symbolic criminal law as a tool for social recognition—particularly by a segment of uninformed progressivism that views such criminalization as a step toward equality for the vulnerable targeted by punitive power—is evident. Yet, for a more attentive observer rooted in practice, the sense of incompatibility between instrument, object, and intended outcome is unmistakable.

In its opening article, the Bill declares: "Article 1: This law aims to criminalize acts committed against a person due to their condition of poverty, thus referred to as aporophobia."[92] This provision seems to describe a different social reality than Brazil's—one in which poverty would be an exceptional condition, rather than a structural feature that imprisons millions of Brazilians in subhuman conditions. In light of the sweeping scope of this definition and the pervasive socioeconomic inequality in Brazilian society, the term *aporophobia* could well be replaced by *Brazilianophobia*, as we suggested earlier in this essay.

From a dogmatic standpoint, this same provision is equally problematic due to its breadth, which invites the kind of primary criminalization typical of selective penal law. Its open-ended wording allows ample discretion for interpretation at the point of application, ultimately reinforcing selective stereotypes that determine what counts as aporophobia. It does not take a sophisticated hermeneutic exercise to anticipate the selective deployment of this concept—especially given its vagueness, which already undermines the principle of *lex certa* in penal law.[93]

Article 2 of the Bill introduces a new aggravating factor into Article 121 of the Penal Code, related to homicide. The proposed item V-A would read: "V-A—[Homicide] as a result of a feeling of hatred for the victim's condition of poverty."[94]

Yet, the statistics on the abyssal legal-criminal selectivity of lethal violence in Brazil confirm that nearly all victims belong to the very social group constructed as pariahs by the media and previously described here. The mere existence of a criminal provision prohibiting homicide has not been sufficient to curb the extreme lethality of Brazil's punitive power—lethality overwhelmingly linked to poverty. Even from a dogmatic viewpoint, this new aggravation appears useless.

It is also notable that the proposal seems to disregard item II of the same Article 121, which already punishes homicide committed for a *futile reason* with the same penalty proposed for *aporophobic homicide*. If hatred toward the poor is not considered a futile motive, or if it is and the legislative measure is unnecessary, then we are merely dealing with symbolic legislation that yields effects contrary to those promised.

What is particularly striking is that, although state punitive power is the main driver of lethal violence in Brazil—whether through direct action or by promoting violence via criminalizing narratives—the proposed Bill fails to even acknowledge this. There is no reference whatsoever to potential state responsibility in the perpetration of aporophobia.

While this omission may have little practical impact—given that punitive power in Brazil has always been structurally aporophobic, aligned with the logic of power/property—it does reveal a lack of genuine commitment to the issue on the part of those defending aporophobia as a criminological-critical concept.

The Bill also proposes, in Article 129 of the Penal Code (bodily harm), a new §13: "If the injury is committed as a result of a feeling of hatred for the victim's condition of poverty, the penalty is increased by one-third."[95] Given the patterns of victimization in Brazil and throughout the region[96]—disproportionately affecting socially vulnerable individuals, predominantly Black and Brown residents of peripheral neighborhoods—this aggravation would apply to virtually all victims of bodily harm. That alone signals its inadequacy: As we have already noted, what applies to everything ultimately applies to nothing, particularly in criminal law, which demands guarantees and precision.

Finally, the Bill proposes an amendment to §3 of Article 140 of the Penal Code (insult), "If the insult consists of the use of elements referring to race, color, ethnicity, religion, origin, or the condition of an elderly or disabled person, or *their condition of poverty*."[97]

It seems evident that motivations far removed from the protection of vulnerable individuals underlie this legislative proposal. It resembles a dissonance between latent and manifest content, leaving it unclear which element represents the latent goal: symbolic legitimation or genuine concern.

Moreover, one must question the legitimacy of penal types aimed at "protecting" the legal good of honor—especially from the standpoint of a minimal criminal law. It seems inappropriate to use criminal law to safeguard this value, particularly when monetary reparations might prove more effective, assuming the objective is not revenge or public shaming—goals that should not fall under the purview of criminal law.[98]

The notion of protecting the *honor* of vulnerable individuals—social pariahs, not recognized as persons, often lacking formal education, living in unsanitary conditions, and regularly hunting to feed Brazil's penal statistics—strikes us as sociologically and criminologically off base. This is not to say these individuals are undeserving of protection. Quite the opposite, a genuine rescue of their dignity is urgently needed—but not through symbolic measures with little or no effect. At best, the criminal response would not materialize; at worst, it would target other vulnerable individuals, reinforcing the same selective logic.

Thus, even if proposed in good faith—which we presume—the Bill ultimately contributes to the abyssal selectivity of punitive power in Brazil. It accelerates the movement toward an increasingly symbolic and selective criminal law, failing to incorporate either a structural analysis or a systemic critique.

4.14 Criminological Intersectionality and Epistemologies of the South: Far Beyond Aporophobia

To see and make others see the selectivity of our punitive power in a critical, reflective, and emancipatory way, a local analysis is indispensable. This does not imply determinism of any kind, nor linear movements that contribute little to overcoming complex issues such as those involving criminal knowledge and punitive power.

We do not advocate for replacing one determinism (poverty) with another (racial matrix) in the criminological construction of reflections and alternatives to the current movement of an uncontrolled penal system in Brazil. Rather, we understand that our punitive power exhibits a certain racist preference rooted in the slaveholding matrix that continues to structurally permeate Brazilian society, its institutions, and its subjects.

This slaveholding scar is the hermeneutic key to interpreting our abyssal legal-criminal selectivity—in the sense that, without it, it becomes impossible to understand, criticize, or propose viable alternatives to such an unchecked movement of punitive power.

Nevertheless, as already inferred from our frank belief in the epistemological value of interdisciplinarity, this initial stance must be enriched by all the socio-political segments that directly or indirectly reverberate in punitive power—something like a crossroads and its roads which, in a geographical dance, come together to form a whole, even if with well-defined and independent parts.

In this sense, we may speak of a movement of intersectionality—albeit with criminological features.[99] This intersectionality, to which we refer, would be: "a lens through which you can see where the energy comes and collides, where it interposes and intersects. It's not simply a racial problem here, a gender problem there, and a class or LGBTQ problem over there. Often, this structure erases what happens to people who are subject to all these things."[100]

On this stance—which is also political, like every theory or method—we could also say that it is a way of interpreting the world in an interdisciplinary manner, understood as something that requires us to "step out of the particular boxes that hinder global struggles."[101]

Intersectionality thus seems suitable for constructing the heuristic tools capable of interpreting our punitive power from the most diverse perspectives, with our slaveholding heritage as the hermeneutic key. In fact, intersectionality itself leads us to identify, because of its interdisciplinary nature, this historical scar as the interpretive key to understanding our penal system.

To this, we add the claim for a *southern epistemology*, in which local knowledge and critical, reflective thought about our own reality play a fundamental role in interpreting our practical and theoretical problems. It is a movement of production and validation of heuristic tools from the South, grounded in the belief that this is the most appropriate way to deeply comprehend our singular problems, such as legal-penal and criminological ones.

All of this leads to an "ecology of knowledge"[102] capable of unveiling the invisible and the unprecedented, so that this knowledge can be converted into emancipatory practices, always socially responsible—for, in this theoretical (and political) perspective, there is no room for scientific extractivism. That is, within the idea of epistemologies of the South, scientific results must foster local and liberating social transformations. Thus, it may be said that, "southern epistemologies creatively reflect on this reality to offer a critical diagnosis of the present, which obviously has as its constitutive element the possibility of reconstructing, formulating, and legitimating alternatives for a more just and free society."[103]

Both theoretical claims of the aforementioned critical movements are valid for addressing the unchecked exercise of punitive power—even if they are not the only ones capable of casting realistic light on our daily tragedy of the violent and abyssal selective operation of the penal system's executive agencies.

Both intersectionality and southern epistemologies are stances that are not only useful but necessary for criminological knowledge, so as to avoid simplifications and determinisms in the analysis of our specific punitive power. These theoretical tools, in conjunction with others we have discussed throughout this work, are what have allowed us to perceive the methodological and emancipatory inadequacy of aporophobia as a suitable criminological-critical concept.

Notes

1. Sousa Santos, B. (1997). Por uma concepção multicultural de direitos humanos. *Revista Crítica de Ciências Sociais*, n. 48, pp. 11–32.; Ferrajoli, L. (2019). Crimini di sistema. *Rivista online del Centro Interdipartimentale di Ricerca Franco Fortini dell'Università degli Studi di Siena*, pp. 1–10.
2. Castro, L. A. de (1990). La política criminal y la nueva criminología en América Latina. In *Criminología en América Latina*. Roma: Instituto Interregional de Naciones Unidas para la Investigación sobre el Delito y la Justicia—UNICRI, p. 32.
3. Dias Dos Santos, Í. (2025). Normative Tatbestandsmerkmale im Strafrecht. Gedanken über das Verständnis normativ-rechtlicher Elemente in komplexen und multikulturellen Gesellschaften. *Goltdammer's Archiv für Strafrecht (GA)*, v. 172 (in press).
4. Sack, F. (1980). Die Kriminologie auf fremdem Boden. In Lädemen, K. & Sack, F. (Hrsg.), *Vom Nutzen und Nachteil der Sozialwissenschaften für das Strafrecht*. Frankfurt am Main:Suhrkamp Verlag, pp. 35 ff.; Sousa Santos, B. (2017). *Justicia entre saberes: Epistemologías del Sur contra el epistemicidio*. Madrid: Morata, pp. 159 ff.
5. Aniyar de Castro, L. (1987). *Criminología de la liberación*. Maracaibo: Editorial de la Universidad del Zulia, p. 42.; Aniyar de Castro, L. (1977). *Criminología de la reacción social*. Maracaibo: Universidad del Zulia, pp. 9 ff.; Aniyar de Castro, L. (1982). *La realidad contra los mitos. Reflexiones críticas en criminología*. Maracaibo: Universidad del Zulia, pp. 11 ff.; Aniyar de Castro, L. (2003). *Entre la dominación y el miedo. Nueva criminología y nueva política criminal*. Mérida: Ediciones Nuevo Siglo, pp. 39 ff.; Aniyar de Castro, L. (2010). *Criminología de los derechos humanos: criminología axiológica como política criminal*. Buenos Aires: Del Puerto, pp. 32 ff.; Aniyar de Castro, L. (1981). *Conocimiento y orden social: criminología como legitimación y criminología como liberación (proposiciones para una criminología latinoamericana como teoría crítica del control social)*. Maracaibo: Universidad del Zulia, pp. 33 ff.; Aniyar de Castro, L. (2009). La criminología crítica en el siglo XXI como criminología de los derechos humanos y la contrarreforma humanística o las teorías criminológicas no son inocentes. *Revista Brasileira de Ciências Criminais*, n. 76, pp. 289 ff. Aniyar de Castro, L. (1969). *Victimología. Consideraciones generales*. Maracaibo: Universidad del Zulia, pp. 39 ff.; Aniyar de Castro, L. & Codino, R. (2013). *Manual de Criminología Sociopolítica*. Buenos Aires: Ediar, pp. 303 ff.

6. Del Olmo, R. (1979). *Ruptura criminológica*. Caracas: Universidad Central de Venezuela, p. 163.; Del Olmo, R. (1981). *América Latina y su criminología*. México: Siglo Veintiuno Editores, pp. 9 ff.; Del Olmo, R. (1990). *Segunda ruptura criminológica*. Caracas: Universidad Central de Venezuela, pp. 13 ff.; Del Olmo, R. (1975). *La socio-política de las drogas*. Caracas: Universidad Central de Venezuela, pp. 13 ff.; Del Olmo, R. (1992). *¿Prohibir o domesticar? Políticas de drogas en América Latina*. Caracas: Editorial Nueva Sociedad, pp. 15 ff.
7. Bricola, F. (1997). *Politica criminale e scienza del diritto penale*. Bologna: Società Editrice il Mulino, pp. 177–188.
8. Zaffaroni, R. (1982). *Política criminal latinoamericana: perspectivas—disyuntivas*. Buenos Aires: Editorial Hammurabi, pp. 31 ff.
9. Pérez Cepeda, A. I. (2010). La criminalización de la pobreza y la expansión de la población carcelaria. *Revista Brasileira de Ciências Criminais*, ano 18, n. 82, pp. 257–294.
10. IIDH—Instituto Interamericano de Derechos Humanos. (1986). *Sistemas penales y derechos humanos en América Latina (Informe final)*. Documento final del programa de investigación desarrollado por el Instituto Interamericano de Derechos Humanos (1982–1986), coordinador Profesor Doctor Raúl Zaffaroni. Buenos Aires: Ediciones Depalma, p. 459.; IIDH—Instituto Interamericano de Derechos Humanos. (1984). *Sistemas penales y derechos humanos en América Latina (Primer Informe)*. Documentos y cuestionarios elaborados para el seminario de San José, Costa Rica, 11 al 15 de julio de 1983, redactados por el coordinador Profesor Doctor Raúl Zaffaroni. Buenos Aires: Ediciones Depalma, pp. 50 ff.
11. Longobardo, C. (2013). *L'infedeltà patrimoniale. Profili sistematici e di politica criminale*. Napoli: Edizioni Scientifiche Italiane, pp. 18 ff.
12. Zaffaroni, R. (1993). *Criminología: aproximación desde un margen*. Bogotá: Temis, p. 19.
13. Muñoz Conde, F. (1989). La criminología de la liberación: ¿una nueva criminología? *Revista Doctrina Penal*, año 12, pp. 456 ff.; Aniyar de Castro, L. & Codino, R. (2013). *Manual de Criminología Sociopolítica*. Buenos Aires: Ediar, p. 264.; Aniyar de Castro, L. (1987). *Criminología de la liberación*. Maracaibo: Editorial de la Universidad del Zulia, pp. 5 ff.
14. Del Olmo, R. (1987). *Cuando la realidad no existe (El asalto al Palacio de Justicia, Bogotá, Colombia, 6 y 7 de noviembre de 1985)*. Trabajo inédito mecanografiado. Caracas: mayo de 1987.
15. Science in general—and social science in particular—tends to reject the incorporation of heuristic elements that diverge from its dogmas, almost always sacralized by the epistemologies of the North. In critical analyses such as the one undertaken in this work, the path can only be that of epistemic renewal through the incorporation of heuristic elements from the South: a confluence of critical knowledges that does not delegitimize other forms of understanding by appealing to the well-worn pretext of scientificity. In this sense, the Foucauldian question remains holistically pertinent: "What types of knowledge do you want to disqualify when you call yourself a science?" (Foucault, M. (2019). *Microfísica del poder*. Buenos Aires: Siglo Veintiuno Editores, p. 220.; On the classic debate about the scientificity of criminology see Petrocelli, B. (1957). Diritto penale e criminologia. *Rivista Italiana di Diritto e Procedura Penale*, n. 4, v. 10, p. 688.)
16. Novoa Monreal, E. (1985). Desorientación epistemológica en la criminología crítica. *Revista Doctrina Penal*, año 8, pp. 263 ff.; Aniyar de Castro, L. (1986). "El jardín de al lado", o respondiendo a Novoa sobre la criminología crítica. *Revista Doctrina Penal*, año 9, pp. 305 ff.; Novoa Monreal, E. (1986). Lo que hay al lado no es un jardín: mi réplica a Lola Aniyar de Castro. *Revista Doctrina Penal*, año 9, pp. 315 ff.; Muñoz Conde, F. (1989). La criminología de la liberación: ¿una nueva criminología? *Revista Doctrina Penal*, año 12, p. 456.

17. Aniyar de Castro, L. (recop.) (1974). *Los rostros de la violencia. XXIII Curso Internacional de Criminología*. Maracaibo: Universidad del Zulia, pp. 15 ff.; Aniyar de Castro, L. (ed.) (1990). *Criminología en América Latina*. Roma: Unicri, pp. 9 ff.; Zaffaroni, R. (Dir.) (2014). *Ciencias penales desde el sur: Segundo Congreso Latinoamericano de derecho penal y criminología*. Buenos Aires: Infojus, pp. xxi ff.; IBCCRIM—Instituto Brasileiro de Ciências Criminais. (2017). *IBCCRIM 25 anos*. Belo Horizonte: D'Plácido, pp. 10 ff.; Sozzo, M. (coord.) (2006). *Reconstruyendo las criminologías críticas*. Buenos Aires: Ad-Hoc, pp. 9 ff.
18. Seabra Santos, F. & Almeida-Filho, N. de. (2012). *A quarta missão da universidade: internacionalização universitária na sociedade do conhecimento*. Coimbra: Imprensa da Universidade de Coimbra, pp. 27 ff.; Buarque, C. (1994). *A aventura da universidade*. São Paulo: Unesp / Rio de Janeiro: Paz e Terra, pp. 13 ff.; Ribeiro, D. (1969). *A Universidade necessária*. Rio de Janeiro: Paz e Terra, pp. 167 ff.; Teixeira, A. (2005). *Ensino superior no Brasil: análise e interpretação de sua evolução até 1969*. Rio de Janeiro: EDUFRJ, pp. 178 ff.; Gimbernat Ordeig, E. (2018). *El Derecho penal en el mundo*. Navarra: Aranzadi, pp. 319 ff.; Díaz y García Conlledo, M. & García Amado, J. A. (2012). La Universidad española y sus Facultades de Derecho. Diagnóstico y propuestas de tratamiento. *Teoría & Derecho: Revista de Pensamiento Jurídico*, n. 11, pp. 277–294.; Stefani, G. (1998). L'università italiana di fronte ai mutamenti demografici e sociali. In *UNISA. Fraterna Munera. Studi in Onore di Luigi Amirante*. Salerno: Università degli Studi di Ferrara e Università degli Studi di Salerno, pp. 427 ff.
19. Camargo, A. L. C. (1996). Contradições da modernidade e Direito penal. *Revista Brasileira de Ciências Criminais*, v. 4, n. 16, pp. 115–117.; Berdugo Gómez de la Torre, I. (2007). Estudiar Derecho hoy. In Pérez Álvarez, F. (Dir.), *Universitas Vitae: Homenaje a Ruperto Núñez Barbero*. Salamanca: Ediciones Universidad de Salamanca, pp. 77 ff.; Zúñiga Rodríguez, L. (2018). *Proyecto Docente e Investigador*. Presentado en cumplimiento de la normativa vigente relativa al concurso a plaza de Catedrática de Derecho penal de la Universidad de Salamanca.
20. Berdugo Gómez de la Torre, I. & Zaffaroni, R. (1994). *Los Códigos Penales Iberoamericanos* n. 1 (presentación e introducción, respectivamente). Santa Fe de Bogotá: Forum Pacis, pp. 13 ff.
21. Tavares, J. (2018). *Fundamento de teoria do delito*. Florianópolis: Tirant lo Blanch, pp. 366 ff.; Cirino dos Santos, J. (2010). *Direito penal. Parte Geral*. Florianópolis: Conceito Editorial, pp. 419 ff.; Batista, N. (1990). *Introdução crítica ao direito penal brasileiro*. Rio de Janeiro: Editora Revan, pp. 17 ff.
22. Santos, M. (1997). O intelectual e a universidade estagnada. *Revista Adusp*, n. 11, p. 20.
23. Muñoz Conde, F. (1985). *Derecho penal y control social*. Jerez: Fundación Universitaria de Jerez, p. 41.
24. Szabo, D. (1978). *Criminologie et politique criminelle*. Paris: Vrin, pp. 106 ff.
25. Sousa Santos, B. de (1997). Por uma concepção multicultural de direitos humanos. *Revista Crítica de Ciências Sociais*, n. 48, pp. 11–32.; Ferrajoli, L. (2019). Crimini di Sistema. *Rivista online del Centro Interdipartimentale di Ricerca Franco Fortini dell'Università degli Studi di Siena*, pp. 1–10.; Ferrajoli, L. (2014). Criminología, criminalidad global y derecho penal. El debate epistemológico en la Criminología contemporánea. In Rivera Beiras, I. (coord.), *Delitos de los Estados, de los Mercados y daño social: debates en criminología crítica y sociología jurídico-penal*. Barcelona: Anthropos, pp. 81–96.
26. Garland, D. (2011). *The culture of control. Crime and social order in contemporary society*. New York: Oxford University Press.
27. Melossi, D. (2019). Prefazione. In Baratta, A., *Criminologia critica e critica del diritto penale. Introduzione alla sociologia giuridico-penale*. Milano: Meltemi, pp. 13–21.
28. Zaffaroni, R. & Dias Dos Santos, Í. (2019). *La nueva crítica criminológica: criminología en tiempos de totalitarismo financiero*. Valencia: Tirant lo Blanch, 2020.;

Rivera Beiras, I. (2017). *Descarcelación. Principios para una política pública de reducción de la cárcel (desde un garantismo radical).* Valencia: Tirant lo Blanch, pp. 60 ff.

29. IIDH—Instituto Interamericano de Derechos Humanos. (1993). *Muertes anunciadas.* Bogotá: Temis, p. 10.
30. Zaffaroni, R. (2010). *Crímenes de masa.* Buenos Aires: Ediciones Madres de Plaza de Mayo, pp. 27 ff.
31. Torrente, D. (2001). *Desviación y delito.* Madrid: Alianza Editorial, p. 18.
32. Dimenstein, G. (1990). *A guerra dos meninos. Assassinatos de menores no Brasil.* São Paulo: Brasiliense, p. 14.
33. Moraes, E. (1927). *Criminalidade da infância e da adolescência.* Rio de Janeiro: Francisco Alves Ed., p. 9.
34. Barbagli, M. (1995). *L'occasione e l'uomo ladro. Furti e rapine in Italia.* Bologna: Società Editrice il Mulino, pp. 61 ff.
35. Sousa Santos, B. (2018). *O fim do império cognitivo. A afirmação das Epistemologias do Sul.* Coimbra: Edições Almedina, pp. 19 ff.; Sousa Santos, B. (2007). Para além do pensamento abissal: das linhas globais a uma ecologia de saberes. *Revista Crítica de Ciências Sociais*, n. 78, pp. 3–46.; Sousa Santos, B. & Meneses, M. P. (Orgs.) (2018). *Epistemologias do Sul.* Coimbra: Edições Almedina / CES, pp. 73 ff.; Sousa Santos, B. (2002). Para uma sociologia das ausências e uma sociologia das emergências. *Revista Crítica de Ciências Sociais*, n. 63, pp. 237–280.
36. Sousa Santos, B. (2002). Para uma sociologia das ausências e uma sociologia das emergências. *Revista Crítica de Ciências Sociais*, n. 63, pp. 237–280.
37. Dias Dos Santos, Í. (2018). *En busca de la justicia restaurativa. Un cambio de paradigma en el Derecho Penal de Garantías.* Buenos Aires: BdeF, pp. 68 ff.
38. Londoño Berrío, H. L. (2016). *Sistemas punitivos y derechos humanos: el caso de la Comuna 13 de Medellín—Colombia.* Bogotá: Ediciones Jurídicas Andrés Morales, pp. xxiii ff.
39. Aniyar de Castro, L. (1987). *Criminología de la liberación.* Maracaibo: Editorial de la Universidad del Zulia, pp. 96 ff.
40. Cano, I. & Rojido, E. (2017). Introducción: la singularidad de la violencia letal en América Latina. *Revista CIDOB d'Afers Internacionals*, n. 116, pp. 7 ff.
41. Chiari Gonçalves, V. (2014). *Tortura e cultura policial no Brasil contemporâneo.* Rio de Janeiro: Lumen Juris.
42. Schoenfeld, H. (2018). *Building the Prison State: Race and the Politics of Mass Incarceration.* Chicago: University of Chicago Press, pp. 122 ff.; Malaguti Batista, V. (2011). *Introdução crítica à criminologia brasileira.* Rio de Janeiro: Revan, pp. 99 ff.; Lourenço, L. C. & Rocha Gomes, G. L. (Orgs.) (2013). *Prisões e punição no Brasil contemporâneo.* Salvador, pp. 7 ff.; Carvalho, S. de. (2018). O encarceramento seletivo da juventude negra brasileira: a decisiva contribuição do Poder Judiciário. In Calazans, M. E. de, Castro, M. G. & Piñeiro, E. da S. (Orgs.), *América Latina: Corpos, Trânsitos e Resistências. Volume II.* Porto Alegre: Editora Fi, pp. 495–525.; Pavarini, M. (2010). O encarceramento de massa. In Vieira Abramovay, P. & Malaguti Batista, V. (Orgs.), *Depois do grande encarceramento.* Rio de Janeiro: Revan, pp. 293–312.; Pavarini, M. (2013). *Governare la penalità: struttura sociale, processi decisionali e discorsi pubblici sulla pena.* Bologna: Bononia University Press (numero monografico della *Rivista Studi e materiali di diritto penale*, n. 3/2013), pp. 24 ff.; Pavarini, M. (2004). Processi di ricarcerizzazione nel mondo (ovvero del dominio di un certo punto di vista). *Questione Giustizia*, n. 2/3, pp. 8 ff.; Pérez Cepeda, A. I. (2007). *La seguridad como fundamento de la deriva del derecho penal postmoderno.* Madrid: Iustel, pp. 468 ff.; Wacquant, L. (1999). *Les Prisons de la misère.* Paris: Raisons d'agir, pp. 78 ff.

43. Zúñiga Rodríguez, L. (2001). *Política criminal*. Madrid: Colex, p. 34; Lappi-Seppälä, T. (2011). Explaining imprisonment in Europe. *European Journal of Criminology*, v. 8, n. 4, pp. 303 ff.
44. Carranza, E. (1983). *El preso sin condena en América Latina y el Caribe: estudio comparativo estadístico y legal de treinta países y propuestas para reducir al fenómeno*. San José: ILANUD, p. 23, second note.
45. Ministério da Justiça do Brasil. Departamento Penitenciário Nacional—Sistema Integrado de Informação Penitenciária. (2017). *Infopen*. Brasília, pp. 5 ff.
46. Gonnella, P. & Ruotolo, M. (a cura di) (2016). *Giustizia e carceri secondo Papa Francesco*. Milano: Editoriale Jaca Book, pp. 95 ff.
47. Pisapia, G. D. (1953). *Reati contro il patrimonio*. Milano: La Goliardica / Edizioni Universitarie—Università degli Studi di Milano (Facoltà di Giurisprudenza), p. 9.
48. Zaffaroni, R. & Dias Dos Santos, Í. (2020). *La nueva crítica criminológica. Criminología en tiempos de totalitarismo financiero*. Valencia: Tirant lo Blanch, pp. 55 ff.
49. Stiglitz, J. (2018). *Globalization and its discontents revisited. Anti-globalization in the era of Trump*. New York: Norton & Company, pp. 8 ff.; Stiglitz, J. (2007). *Making globalization work*. New York: Norton & Company, pp. 50 ff.
50. Tavares, J. (1997). A crescente legislação penal e os discursos de emergência. *Discursos Sediciosos: Crime, Direito e Sociedade*, n. 4, v. 2, pp. 44 ff.
51. Gil Villa, F. (2013). *Introducción a las teorías criminológicas. Por qué rompemos con la norma*. Madrid: Tecnos, pp. 130 ff.
52. Zaffaroni, R. & Dias Dos Santos, Í. (2020). *La nueva crítica criminológica. Criminología en tiempos de totalitarismo financiero*. Valencia: Tirant lo Blanch, pp. 77 ff.
53. Brandariz García, J. Á. (2014). *El gobierno de la penalidad. La complejidad de la política criminal contemporánea*. Madrid: Editorial Dykinson, pp. 92 ff.
54. Martin, H.-P. & Schumann, H. (1996). *Die Globalisierungsfalle: Der Angriff auf Demokratie und Wohlstand*. Hamburg: Rowohlt Verlag, pp. 9 ff.
55. Picó, J. (1987). *Teorías sobre el Estado del Bienestar*. Madrid: Siglo Veintiuno de España, pp. 13 ff; Alberich Nistal, T. & Amezcua Aguilar, T. (2017). Desigualdad, clases sociales y sociedad de los tres tercios. *Sistema: Revista de Ciencias Sociales*, n. 245, pp. 17 ff.; Mishra, R. (2014). *Welfare State Capitalist Society*. London and New York: Routledge, pp. 97 ff.
56. Cantarero Bandrés, R. (1990). Seguridad ciudadana. Constitución. Derecho penal. *Cuadernos de Política Criminal*, n. 42, p. 528.
57. Martin, H.-P. & Schumann, H. (1996). *Die Globalisierungsfalle: Der Angriff auf Demokratie und Wohlstand*. Hamburg: Rowohlt Verlag, pp. 9 ff. Initially, the authors refer to a "20:80 society" (*The 20:80 Society*), but later acknowledge the possibility of including a small additional portion within that 20% of included individuals. For this reason, we prefer the 30:70 formula, which we consider mathematically more accurate in describing this debilitating hurricane affecting democracies. We develop this point in greater detail in: Zaffaroni, R. & Dias Dos Santos, Í. (2020). *La nueva crítica criminológica. Criminología en tiempos de totalitarismo financiero*. Valencia: Tirant lo Blanch, pp. 77 ff.
58. Tavares, J. (1997). A crescente legislação penal e os discursos de emergência. *Discursos Sediciosos: Crime, Direito e Sociedade*, n. 4, v. 2, pp. 43 ff.
59. García Arán, M. (2008). El discurso mediático sobre la delincuencia y su incidencia en las reformas penales. *Revista Catalana de Seguretat Pública*, v. 18, p. 47.; Fuentes Osorio, J. L. (2005). Los medios de comunicación y el derecho penal. *Revista Electrónica de Ciencia Penal y Criminología*, n. 07–16, p. 5.
60. Goffman, E. (1963). *Stigma. Notes on the management of spoiled identity*. Englewood Cliffs: Prentice-Hall, pp. 41 ff.; Heatherton, T. F., Kleck, R. E., Hebl, M. R. & Hull, J. G. (Eds.) (2003). *The social psychology of stigma*. New York: Guilford Press.

61. Moccia, S. (2011). *La perenne emergenza: tendenze autoritarie nel sistema penale*. Napoli: Edizioni Scientifiche Italiane, p. 100.
62. Zaffaroni, R. & Dias Dos Santos, Í. (2020). *La nueva crítica criminológica. Criminología en tiempos de totalitarismo financiero*. Valencia: Tirant lo Blanch, pp. 10 ff.
63. Stiglitz, J. (2018). *Globalization and its discontents revisited. Anti-globalization in the era of Trump*. New York: Norton & Company, pp. 8 ff.
64. Silva Franco, A. (2001). Breves anotações sobre os crimes patrimoniais. In Shecaira, S. S. (Org.), *Estudos criminais em homenagem a Evandro Lins e Silva: criminalista do século*. São Paulo: Editora Método, pp. 62 ff.
65. Von Mises, L. (2011). *La mentalidad anticapitalista*. Madrid: Unión Editorial, pp. 19 ff.
66. Sousa Santos, B. de (2009). *Sociología jurídica crítica. Para un nuevo sentido común en el derecho*. Madrid: Trotta, pp. 96 ff.
67. Beristain, A. (1982). Concepto y método del Derecho Criminal. In Barbero Santos, M., Cerezo Mir, J., Gimbernat Ordeig, E. & Núñez Barbero, R. (Orgs.), *Estudios penales: libro homenaje al Prof. J. Antón Oneca*. Salamanca: Ediciones Universidad de Salamanca, p. 77.
68. Morrison, W. (2012). *Criminología, civilización y nuevo orden mundial*. Barcelona: Anthropos, pp. 15 ff.
69. Sousa Santos, B. de (2009). *Sociología jurídica crítica. Para un nuevo sentido común en el derecho*. Madrid: Trotta, p. 38.; Santos, M. (2006). *A natureza do espaço: técnica e tempo, razão e emoção*. São Paulo: Edusp, pp. 212 ff.
70. Santos, M. (1996). *A natureza do espaço: técnica e tempo. Razão e emoção*. São Paulo: Hucitec, pp. 51 ff.
71. Castells, M. (1998). *La era de la información. Economía, sociedad y cultura. Volumen I. La sociedad red*. Madrid: Alianza Editorial, p. 28.
72. Castells, M. (1998). *La era de la información. Economía, sociedad y cultura. Volumen I. La sociedad red*. Madrid: Alianza Editorial, p. 59.
73. Garland, D. (2011). *The culture of control. Crime and social order in contemporary society*. New York: Oxford University Press, pp. 27 ff.
74. Simon, J. (2007). *Governing through crime. How the war on crime transformed American democracy and created a culture of fear*. Oxford: Oxford University Press, pp. 13 ff.
75. Wacquant, L. (1999). *Les prisons de la misère*. Paris: Raisons d'agir, pp. 9 ff.; Wacquant, L. (2009). *Punishing the poor: the neoliberal government of social insecurity*. Durham: Duke University Press, pp. 11 ff.
76. Del Olmo, R. (1979). *Ruptura criminológica*. Caracas: Universidad Central de Venezuela, p. 163.
77. Zaffaroni, R. (1993). *Criminología: aproximación desde un margen*. Bogotá: Temis, p. 19.
78. Sousa Santos, B. de (2018). *O fim do império cognitivo. A afirmação das Epistemologias do Sul*. Coimbra: Edições Almedina, pp. 19 ff.; Sousa Santos, B. de & Meneses, M. P. (Orgs.) (2018). *Epistemologias do Sul*. Coimbra: Edições Almedina / CES, pp. 73 ff.
79. Zaffaroni, R. & Santos, Í. D. dos (2020). *La nueva crítica criminológica. Criminología en tiempos de totalitarismo financiero*. Valencia: Tirant lo Blanch, pp. 51 ff.
80. Zaffaroni, R. (1989). *En busca de las penas perdidas: deslegitimación y dogmática jurídico-penal*. Buenos Aires: Ediar, p. 100.
81. Ferrajoli, L. (2018). *Diritto e ragione: teoria del garantismo penale*. Roma: Laterza, pp. 193 ff.
82. Baratta, A. (1979). Criminologia e dogmatica penale. Passato e futuro del modello integrato di scienza penalistica. *La Questione Criminale. Rivista di ricerca e dibattito su devianza e controllo sociale*, anno 5, n. 2, pp. 147–172.; Baratta, A. (1975).

Criminologia liberale e ideologia della difesa sociale. *La Questione Criminale. Rivista di ricerca e dibattito su devianza e controllo sociale*, v. 1, n. 1, pp. 7–61.
83. Baratta, A. (2004). ¿Tiene futuro la criminología crítica? Reflexiones sobre el modelo integrado de las ciencias penales y la interdisciplinariedad externa. In *Criminología y Sistema Penal. Compilación in memoriam*. Buenos Aires: BdeF, p. 142.
84. Girardin, É. (1871). *Du droit de punir*. Paris: Henri Plon Imprimeur-Éditeur, pp. 19 ff.
85. Hassemer, W. (1995). Derecho penal simbólico y protección de bienes jurídicos. In Bustos Ramírez, J. (Dir.), *Pena y Estado*. Santiago de Chile: Editorial Jurídica ConoSur, pp. 23 ff.
86. Baratta, A. (1982). *Criminologia critica e critica del diritto penale. Introduzione alla sociologia giuridicopenale*. Bologna: Società Editrice il Mulino, p. 200.
87. Karam, M. L. (1996). A esquerda punitiva. *Discursos Sediciosos: Crime, Direito e Sociedade*, ano 1, n. 1, p. 86.
88. Karam, M. L. (1996). A esquerda punitiva. *Discursos Sediciosos: Crime, Direito e Sociedade*, ano 1, n. 1, p. 88.
89. Karam, M. L. (1996). A esquerda punitiva. *Discursos Sediciosos: Crime, Direito e Sociedade*, ano 1, n. 1, p. 91.
90. Pérez Cepeda, A. I. (2020). Prólogo. In Rubio, M. B., *Aporofobia y delito: la discriminación socioeconómica como agravante (art. 22, 4ª CP)*. Barcelona: JM Bosch, pp. 18–19.
91. Câmara dos Deputados—Brasil. (2020). *Projeto de Lei n.º 3271/20*. Brasília: Câmara dos Deputados, p. 5.
92. Câmara dos Deputados—Brasil. (2020). *Projeto de Lei n.º 3271/20*. Brasília: Câmara dos Deputados, p. 5.
93. Moccia, S. (2001). *La 'Promessa non Mantenuta'. Ruolo e prospettive del principio di determinatezza/tassatività nel sistema penale italiano*. Napoli: Edizioni Scientifiche Italiane, pp. 13 ff.
94. Câmara dos Deputados—Brasil. (2020). *Projeto de Lei n.º 3271/20*. Brasília: Câmara dos Deputados, p. 1.
95. Câmara dos Deputados—Brasil. (2020). *Projeto de Lei n.º 3271/20*. Brasília: Câmara dos Deputados, p. 1.
96. Zaffaroni, R., Alagia, A. & Slokar, A. (2005). *Derecho penal. Parte general*. Buenos Aires: Ediar, pp. 7–18.
97. Câmara dos Deputados—Brasil. (2020). *Projeto de Lei n.º 3271/20*. Brasília: Câmara dos Deputados, p. 1.
98. Oliveira Filho, N. M. de & Prado, A. R. M. (2018). O problema da vingança privada (autotutela): entre o minimalismo garantista e o abolicionismo radical. *Revista de Criminologias e Políticas Criminais*, v. 4, n. 1, pp. 61 ff.
99. Althoff, M. (2010). Intersektionalität. Ein neues Paradigma zur Erfassung sozialer Ungleichheit im Strafrecht? In Temme, G. & Künzel, C. (Orgs.), *Hat Strafrecht ein Geschlecht?*. Bielefeld: transcript Verlag, pp. 255 ff.
100. Carbado, D. W., Crenshaw, K. W., Mays, V. M. & Tomlinson, B. (2013). Intersectionality: Mapping the movements of a theory. *Du Bois Review: Social Science Research on Race*, v. 10, n. 2, pp. 303–312.
101. Akotirene, C. (2018). *O que é interseccionalidade?* São Paulo: Pólen, p. 29.
102. Sousa Santos, B. (2010). *Descolonizar el saber y reinventar el poder*. Montevideo: Ediciones Trilce, pp. 49 ff.
103. Sousa Santos, B. (2018). *Introducción: las epistemologías del sur*. Barcelona: CIDOB, p. 14.

Bibliography

Akotirene, C. (2018). *O que é interseccionalidade?* Pólen.

Alberich Nistal, T., & Amezcua Aguilar, T. (2017). Desigualdad, clases sociales y sociedad de los tres tercios. *Sistema: Revista de Ciencias Sociales*, 245.

Althoff, M. (2010). Intersektionalität. Ein neues Paradigma zur Erfassung sozialer Ungleichheit im Strafrecht? In G. Temme & C. Künzel (Eds..), *Hat Strafrecht ein Geschlecht?* Transcript Verlag.

Aniyar de Castro, L. (1969). *Victimología. Consideraciones generales*. Universidad del Zulia.

Aniyar de Castro, L. (1974). *Los rostros de la violencia. XXIII Curso Internacional de Criminología*. Universidad del Zulia.

Aniyar de Castro, L. (1977). *Criminología de la reacción social*. Universidad del Zulia.

Aniyar de Castro, L. (1981). *Conocimiento y orden social: criminología como legitimación y criminología como liberación (proposiciones para una criminología latinoamericana como teoría crítica del control social)*. Universidad del Zulia.

Aniyar de Castro, L. (1982). *La realidad contra los mitos. Reflexiones críticas en criminología*. Universidad del Zulia.

Aniyar de Castro, L. (1986). "El jardín de al lado", o respondiendo a Novoa sobre la criminología crítica. *Revista Doctrina Penal*, año 9.

Aniyar de Castro, L. (1987). *Criminología de la liberación*. Editorial de la Universidad del Zulia.

Aniyar de Castro, L. (1990). La política criminal y la nueva criminología en América Latina. In *Criminología en América Latina*. Instituto Interregional de Naciones Unidas Para la Investigación sobre el Delito y la Justicia – UNICRI.

Aniyar de Castro, L. (ed.). (1990). *Criminología en América Latina*. Unicri.

Aniyar de Castro, L. (2003). *Entre la dominación y el miedo. Nueva criminología y nueva política criminal*. Ediciones Nuevo Siglo.

Aniyar de Castro, L. (2009). La criminología crítica en el siglo XXI como criminología de los derechos humanos y la contrarreforma humanística o las teorías criminológicas no son inocentes. *Revista Brasileira de Ciências Criminais, 76.*

Aniyar de Castro, L. (2010). *Criminología de los derechos humanos: criminología axiológica como política criminal*. Del Puerto.

Aniyar de Castro, L., & Codino, R. (2013). *Manual de Criminología Sociopolítica*. Ediar.

Baratta, A. (1975). Criminologia liberale e ideologia della difesa sociale. *La Questione Criminale. Rivista di Ricerca e Dibattito su Devianza e Controllo Sociale, 1*(1).

Baratta, A. (1979). Criminologia e dogmatica penale. Passato e futuro del modello integrato di scienza penalistica. *La Questione Criminale. Rivista di Ricerca e Dibattito su Devianza e Controllo Sociale, Anno 5, 2.*

Baratta, A. (1982). *Criminologia Critica e Critica Del Diritto Penale. Introduzione Alla Sociologia Giuridicopenale*. Società Editrice il Mulino.

Baratta, A. (2004). ¿Tiene futuro la criminología crítica? Reflexiones sobre el modelo integrado de las ciencias penales y la interdisciplinariedad externa. In *Criminología Y Sistema Penal. Compilación in Memoriam*. BdeF.

Barbagli, M. (1995). *L'occasione E L'uomo Ladro. Furti E Rapine in Italia*. Società Editrice il Mulino.

Batista, N. (1990). *Introdução crítica ao direito penal brasileiro*. Editora Revan.

Berdugo Gómez de la Torre, I. (2007). Estudiar Derecho hoy. In F. Pérez Álvarez (Dir.), *Universitas Vitae: Homenaje a Ruperto Núñez Barbero*. Ediciones Universidad de Salamanca.

Berdugo Gómez de la Torre, I., & Zaffaroni, R. (1994). Los Códigos Penales Iberoamericanos 1 *(Presentación E Introducción, Respectivamente). Santa Fe de Bogotá*: Forum Pacis.

Beristain, A. (1982). Concepto y método del Derecho Criminal. In M. Barbero Santos, J. Cerezo Mir, E. Gimbernat Ordeig, & R. Núñez Barbero (Eds..), *Estudios Penales: Libro Homenaje Al Prof. J. Antón Oneca*. Ediciones Universidad de Salamanca.

Brandariz García, J. Á. (2014). *El Gobierno de la Penalidad. La Complejidad de la Política Criminal Contemporánea*. Editorial Dykinson.
Bricola, F. (1997). *Politica criminale e scienza del diritto penale*. Società Editrice il Mulino.
Buarque, C. (1994). *A Aventura da Universidade*. Unesp/Rio de Janeiro: Paz e Terra.
Câmara dos Deputados – Brasil. (2020). *Projeto de Lei N.º 3271/20*. Câmara dos Deputados.
Camargo, A. L. C. (1996). Contradições da modernidade e Direito penal. *Revista Brasileira de Ciências Criminais*, *4*(16).
Cano, I., & Rojido, E. (2017). Introducción: La singularidad de la violencia letal en América Latina. *Revista CIDOB d'Afers Internacionals, 116*.
Cantarero Bandrés, R. (1990). Seguridad ciudadana. Constitución. Derecho penal. *Cuadernos de Política Criminal, 42*.
Carbado, D. W., Crenshaw, K. W., Mays, V. M., & Tomlinson, B. (2013). Intersectionality: Mapping the movements of a theory. *Du Bois Review: Social Science Research on Race, 10* (2).
Carranza, E. (1983). *El preso sin condena en América Latina y el Caribe: estudio comparativo estadístico y legal de treinta países y propuestas para reducir al fenómeno*. ILANUD.
Carvalho, S. D. (2018). O encarceramento seletivo da juventude negra brasileira: A decisiva contribuição do Poder Judiciário. In M. E. D. Calazans, M. G. Castro, & E. D. S. Piñeiro (Orgs.), *América Latina: Corpos, Trânsitos E Resistências* (Vol. II). Editora Fi.
Castells, M. (1998). *La era de la información. Economía, sociedad y cultura. Volumen I. La sociedad red*. Alianza Editorial.
Chiari Gonçalves, V. (2014). *Tortura E Cultura Policial No Brasil Contemporâneo*. Lumen Juris.
Cirino Dos Santos, J. (2010). *Direito penal. Parte Geral*. Conceito Editorial.
Del Olmo, R. (1975). *La socio-política de las drogas*. Universidad Central de Venezuela.
Del Olmo, R. (1979). *Ruptura Criminológica*. Universidad Central de Venezuela.
Del Olmo, R. (1981). *América Latina y su criminología*. Siglo Veintiuno Editores.
Del Olmo, R. (1987). *Cuando la Realidad No Existe (El Asalto Al Palacio de Justicia, Bogotá, Colombia, 6 y 7 de Noviembre de 1985)*. mayo de. Trabajo inédito mecanografiado.
Del Olmo, R. (1990). *Segunda ruptura criminológica*. Universidad Central de Venezuela.
Del Olmo, R. (1992). *¿prohibir o domesticar? Políticas de drogas en América Latina*. Editorial Nueva Sociedad.
Dias Dos Santos, Í. (2018). *En busca de la justicia restaurativa. Un cambio de paradigma en el derecho penal de Garantías*. BdeF.
Dias Dos Santos, Í. (2025). Normative Tatbestandsmerkmale im Strafrecht. Gedanken über das Verständnis normativ-rechtlicher Elemente in komplexen und multikulturellen Gesellschaften. *Goltdammer's Archiv Für Strafrecht (GA), 172* (in press).
Díaz, M., Conlledo, G., & Amado, J. A. G. (2012). La Universidad española y sus Facultades de Derecho. Diagnóstico y propuestas de tratamiento. *Teoría & Derecho: Revista de Pensamiento Jurídico, 11*.
Dimenstein, G. (1990). *A Guerra Dos Meninos. Assassinatos de Menores No Brasil*. Brasiliense.
Ferrajoli, L. (2014). Criminología, criminalidad global y derecho penal. El debate epistemológico en la Criminología contemporánea. In I. Rivera Beiras (coord.), *Delitos de Los Estados, de Los Mercados Y Daño Social: Debates En Criminología Crítica Y Sociología Jurídico-penal*. Anthropos.
Ferrajoli, L. (2018). *Diritto E Ragione: Teoria Del Garantismo Penale*. Laterza.
Ferrajoli, L. (2019). Crimini di sistema. *Rivista Online Del Centro Interdipartimentale Di Ricerca Franco Fortini dell'Università Degli Studi Di Siena*.
Foucault, M. (2019). *Microfísica Del Poder*. Siglo Veintiuno Editores.
Fuentes Osorio, J. L. (2005). Los medios de comunicación y el derecho penal. *Revista Electrónica de Ciencia Penal y Criminología*, 07–16.
García Arán, M. (2008). El discurso mediático sobre la delincuencia y su incidencia en las reformas penales. *Revista Catalana de Seguretat Pública, v*, 18.

Garland, D. (2011). *The Culture of Control. Crime and Social Order in Contemporary Society*. Oxford University Press.

Gil Villa, F. (2013). *Introducción a Las Teorías Criminológicas. Por Qué Rompemos Con la Norma*. Tecnos.

Gimbernat Ordeig, E. (2018). *El Derecho Penal En El Mundo*. Aranzadi.

Girardin, É. (1871). *Du Droit de Punir*. Henri Plon Imprimeur-Éditeur.

Goffman, E. (1963). *Stigma. Notes on the Management of Spoiled Identity*. Prentice-Hall.

Gonnella, P., & Ruotolo, M. (2016). *Giustizia E Carceri Secondo Papa Francesco*. Editoriale Jaca Book.

Hassemer, W. (1995). Derecho penal simbólico y protección de bienes jurídicos. In J. Bustos Ramírez (Dir.), *Pena Y Estado*. Editorial Jurídica ConoSur.

Heatherton, T. F., Kleck, R. E., Hebl, M. R., & Hull, J. G. (2003). *The Social Psychology of Stigma*. Guilford Press.

IBCCRIM – Instituto Brasileiro de Ciências Criminais. (2017). *IBCCRIM 25 Anos*. D'Plácido.

IIDH - Instituto Interamericano de Derechos Humanos. (1993). *Muertes Anunciadas*. Temis.

IIDH – Instituto Interamericano de Derechos Humanos. (1984). *Sistemas Penales y Derechos Humanos En América Latina (Primer Informe). Documentos y Cuestionarios Elaborados Para El Seminario de San José, Costa Rica, 11 al 15 de Julio de 1983, Redactados Por El Coordinador Profesor Doctor Raúl Zaffaroni*. Ediciones Depalma.

IIDH – Instituto Interamericano de Derechos Humanos. (1986). *Sistemas Penales y Derechos Humanos En América Latina (Informe Final). Documento Final Del Programa de Investigación Desarrollado Por El Instituto Interamericano de Derechos Humanos (1982–1986), Coordinador Profesor Doctor Raúl Zaffaroni*. Ediciones Depalma.

Karam, M. L. (1996). A esquerda punitiva. *Discursos Sediciosos: Crime, Direito e Sociedade, Ano 1, 1*.

Lappi-Seppälä, T. (2011). Explaining imprisonment in Europe. *European Journal of Criminology*, *8*(4).

Londoño Berrío, H. L. (2016). *Sistemas Punitivos Y Derechos Humanos: El Caso de la Comuna 13 de Medellín - Colombia*. Ediciones Jurídicas Andrés Morales.

Longobardo, C. (2013). *L'infedeltà Patrimoniale. Profili Sistematici e Di Politica Criminale*. Edizioni Scientifiche Italiane.

Lourenço, L. C., Rocha Gomes, G. L. (Orgs.) (2013). *Prisões e Punição No Brasil Contemporâneo*.

Malaguti Batista, V. (2011). *Introdução Crítica À Criminologia Brasileira*. Revan.

Martin, H.-P., & Schumann, H. (1996). *Die Globalisierungsfalle: Der Angriff Auf Demokratie Und Wohlstand*. Rowohlt Verlag.

Melossi, D. (2019). Prefazione. In A. Baratta, *Criminologia Critica e Critica Del Diritto Penale. Introduzione Alla Sociologia Giuridico-penale*. Meltemi.

Ministério da Justiça do Brasil. Departamento Penitenciário Nacional – Sistema Integrado de Informação Penitenciária. (2017). *Infopen*.

Mishra, R. (2014). *Welfare State Capitalist Society*. Routledge.

Moccia, S. (2001). *La 'Promessa Non Mantenuta'. Ruolo e Prospettive Del Principio Di Determinatezza/tassatività Nel Sistema Penale Italiano*. Edizioni Scientifiche Italiane.

Moccia, S. (2011). *La Perenne Emergenza: Tendenze Autoritarie Nel Sistema Penale*. Edizioni Scientifiche Italiane.

Moraes, E. (1927). *Criminalidade da Infância e da Adolescência*. Francisco Alves Ed.

Morrison, W. (2012). *Criminología, Civilización y Nuevo Orden Mundial*. Anthropos.

Muñoz Conde, F. (1985). *Derecho Penal y Control Social*. Fundación Universitaria de Jerez.

Muñoz Conde, F. (1989). La criminología de la liberación: ¿una nueva criminología? *Revista Doctrina Penal*, 12.

Novoa Monreal, E. (1985). Desorientación epistemológica en la criminología crítica. *Revista Doctrina Penal*, 8.

Novoa Monreal, E. (1986). Lo que hay al lado no es un jardín: Mi réplica a Lola Aniyar de Castro. *Revista Doctrina Penal*, 9.

Oliveira Filho, N. M. D., & Prado, A. R. M. (2018). O problema da vingança privada (autotutela): Entre o minimalismo garantista e o abolicionismo radical. *Revista de Criminologias e Políticas Criminais*, *4*(1).

Pavarini, M. (2004). Processi di ricarcerizzazione nel mondo (ovvero del dominio di un certo punto di vista). *Questione Giustizia*, *2*(3).

Pavarini, M. (2010). O encarceramento de massa. In P. Vieira Abramovay & V. Malaguti Batista (Eds..), *Depois Do Grande Encarceramento*. Revan.

Pavarini, M. (2013). *Governare la Penalità: Struttura Sociale, Processi Decisionali e Discorsi Pubblici Sulla Pena*. Bononia University Press. (numero monografico della *Rivista Studi e materiali di diritto penale*, 3/2013).

Pérez Cepeda, A. I. (2007). *La Seguridad Como Fundamento de la Deriva Del Derecho Penal Postmoderno*. Iustel.

Pérez Cepeda, A. I. (2010). La criminalización de la pobreza y la expansión de la población carcelaria. *Revista Brasileira de Ciências Criminais*, *82*, ano 18.

Pérez Cepeda, A. I. (2020). Prólogo. In M. B. Rubio, *Aporofobia y Delito: La Discriminación Socioeconómica Como Agravante (Art. 22, 4ª CP)*. JM Bosch.

Petrocelli, B. (1957). Diritto penale e criminologia. *Rivista Italiana Di Diritto e Procedura Penale*, 10(4).

Picó, J. (1987). *Teorías Sobre El Estado Del Bienestar*. Siglo Veintiuno de España.

Pisapia, G. D. (1953). *Reati Contro Il Patrimonio*. La Goliardica/Edizioni Universitarie – Università degli Studi di Milano (Facoltà di Giurisprudenza).

Ribeiro, D. (1969). *A Universidade Necessária*. Paz e Terra.

Rivera Beiras, I. (2017). *Descarcelación. Principios Para Una Política Pública de Reducción de la Cárcel (Desde Un Garantismo Radical)*. Tirant lo Blanch.

Sack, F. (1980). Die Kriminologie auf fremdem Boden. In K. Lädemen & F. Sack (Eds.), *Vom Nutzen Und Nachteil der Sozialwissenschaften Für Das Strafrecht*. Suhrkamp Verlag.

Santos, M. (1996). *A Natureza Do Espaço: Técnica e Empo. Razão E Emoção*. Hucitec.

Santos, M. (1997). O intelectual e a universidade estagnada. *Revista Adusp*, *11*.

Santos, M. (2006). *A Natureza Do Espaço: Técnica e Tempo, Razão E Emoção*. Edusp.

Schoenfeld, H. (2018). *Building the Prison State: Race and the Politics of Mass Incarceration*. University of Chicago Press.

Seabra Santos, F., & Almeida-Filho, N. D. (2012). *A Quarta Missão da Universidade: Internacionalização Universitária Na Sociedade Do Conhecimento*. Imprensa da Universidade de Coimbra.

Silva Franco, A. (2001). Breves anotações sobre os crimes patrimoniais. In S. S. Shecaira (Ed.), *Estudos Criminais Em Homenagem a Evandro Lins e Silva: Criminalista Do Século*. Editora Método.

Simon, J. (2007). *Governing Through Crime. How the War on Crime Transformed American Democracy and Created a Culture of Fear*. Oxford University Press.

Sousa Santos, B. (1997). Por uma concepção multicultural de direitos humanos. *Revista Crítica de Ciências Sociais*, *48*.

Sousa Santos, B. (1997). Por uma concepção multicultural de direitos humanos. *Revista Crítica de Ciências Sociais*, *48*.

Sousa Santos, B. (2002). Para uma sociologia das ausências e uma sociologia das emergências. *Revista Crítica de Ciências Sociais*, 63.

Sousa Santos, B. (2007). Para além do pensamento abissal: Das linhas globais a uma ecologia de saberes. *Revista Crítica de Ciências Sociais*, *78*.

Sousa Santos, B. (2009). *Sociología Jurídica Crítica. Para Un Nuevo Sentido Común En El Derecho*. Trotta.

Sousa Santos, B. (2010). *Descolonizar El Saber y Reinventar El Poder*. Ediciones Trilce.

Sousa Santos, B. (2017). *Justicia Entre Saberes: Epistemologías Del Sur Contra El Epistemicidio*. Morata.
Sousa Santos, B. (2018). *Introducción: Las Epistemologías Del Sur*. CIDOB.
Sousa Santos, B. (2018). *O Fim Do Império Cognitivo. A Afirmação Das Epistemologias Do Sul*. Edições Almedina.
Sousa Santos, B., & Meneses, M. P. (2018). *Epistemologias Do Sul*. Edições Almedina/CES.
Sousa Santos, B. D., & Meneses, M. P. (2018). *Epistemologias Do Sul*. Edições Almedina/CES.
Sozzo, M. (2006). *Reconstruyendo Las Criminologías Críticas*. Ad-Hoc.
Stefani, G. (1998). L'università italiana di fronte ai mutamenti demografici e sociali. In *UNISA. Fraterna Munera. Studi in Onore Di Luigi Amirante*. Università degli Studi di Ferrara e Università degli Studi di Salerno.
Stiglitz, J. (2007). *Making Globalization Work*. Norton & Company.
Stiglitz, J. (2018). *Globalization and Its Discontents Revisited. Anti-globalization in the Era of Trump*. Norton & Company.
Szabo, D. (1978). *Criminologie Et Politique Criminelle*. Vrin.
Tavares, J. (1997). A crescente legislação penal e os discursos de emergência. *Discursos Sediciosos: Crime, Direito e Sociedade*, 2(4).
Tavares, J. (2018). *Fundamento de Teoria Do Delito*. Tirant lo Blanch.
Teixeira, A. (2005). *Ensino Superior No Brasil: Análise E Interpretação de Sua Evolução Até 1969*. EDUFRJ.
Torrente, D. (2001). *Desviación y Delito*. Alianza Editorial.
Von Mises, L. (2011). *La Mentalidad Anticapitalista*. Unión Editorial.
Wacquant, L. (1999). *Les Prisons de la Misère*. Raisons d'agir.
Wacquant, L. (2009). *Punishing the Poor: The Neoliberal Government of Social Insecurity*. Duke University Press.
Zaffaroni, R. (1982). *Política Criminal Latinoamericana: Perspectivas - Disyuntivas*. Editorial Hammurabi.
Zaffaroni, R. (1989). *En Busca de Las Penas Perdidas: Deslegitimación y Dogmática Jurídico-penal*. Ediar.
Zaffaroni, R. (1993). *Criminología: Aproximación Desde Un Margen*. Temis.
Zaffaroni, R. (2010). *Crímenes de Masa*. Ediciones Madres de Plaza de Mayo.
Zaffaroni, R. (2014). *Ciencias Penales Desde El Sur: Segundo Congreso Latinoamericano de Derecho Penal y Criminología*. Infojus.
Zaffaroni, R., Alagia, A., & Slokar, A. (2005). *Derecho Penal. Parte General*. Ediar.
Zaffaroni, R., & Dias Dos Santos, Í. (2019). *La Nueva Crítica Criminológica: Criminología En Tiempos de Totalitarismo Financiero*. Tirant lo Blanch, 2020.
Zúñiga Rodríguez, L. (2001). *Política Criminal*. Colex.
Zúñiga Rodríguez, L. (2018). *Proyecto Docente e Investigador. Presentado En Cumplimiento de la Normativa Vigente Relativa Al Concurso a Plaza de Catedrática de Derecho Penal de la Universidad de*.

Chapter 5
Final Considerations

Given the critical and reflective nature of this study, its conclusions have been stated throughout the work, as is characteristic of all research that aims to be propositional. In this sense, we present, as final considerations, the main notes derived from the analyses, reflections, and critiques of the object we proposed to study.

Due to its deterministic characteristics and heuristic elements, which are incompatible with the reality of punitive power in Brazil, *aporophobia* does not present itself as an adequate criminological concept from an emancipatory point of view, being, in truth, a kind of failed critical-criminological concept.

Aporophobia, when considered a criminological-critical concept, overlooks the main feeding matrix of punitive power in Brazil: our slaveholding heritage, still present in the political, social, and legal structures of the Brazilian state.

As a criminological-critical concept, *aporophobia* ends up invisibilizing the true matrices that feed legal-penal selectivity, which manifest differently depending on time and place.

This movement functions as a legitimizing strategy of punitive power by placing faith in it as a means to overcome the supposed aversion to the poor. By offering punitive responses to social problems, it reproduces a symbolic and legitimized criminal law.

The devotion of its defenders to criminal law leads to a fundamental and unsurpassable methodological flaw: the belief that a historically unequal instrument (criminal law) can be used to overcome inequality (poverty).

The critique of punitive power carried out through *aporophobia* is, at best, a partial criminological critique, as it neglects the current shift in the global power framework—from productive capitalism to financial totalitarianism.

By ignoring these transformations in global power, *aporophobia* also fails to grasp the emergence of what we have termed "abysmal penal selectivity": a deep intensification of traditional selectivity, increasingly targeting the most vulnerable sectors.

When it adopts poverty as its hermeneutic key, the *aporophobic* approach fails to perceive that abysmal selectivity—both in criminalization and in

Í. Dias Dos Santos, *Aporophobia and Punitive Power in Brazil*,
SpringerBriefs in Criminology,
https://doi.org/10.1007/978-3-032-01753-6_5

incarceration—operates through high-definition racist stereotypes, shaped by historically rooted prejudices and permanently sustained by the media.

As a critical criminological concept, *aporophobia* proves insufficient to grasp the full dimension of the selective imprisonment and criminalization perpetrated by punitive power. Its focus on poverty blinds it to the caste-based criminal policy currently consolidating in Brazil, which divides the population into "levels of citizens" based on racialized stereotypes and prejudices—elements systematically ignored, whether by omission or design, within the aporophobic approach.

From the limited perspective of poverty, as proposed by the notion of *aporophobia* in criminology, it is impossible to see or understand critically the current criminal policy that constructs a "caste of pariahs" as its object. This is a criminal policy of the "other," projecting repressive focus onto those who are no longer seen as people, but as nonpersons—figures blamed, almost biologically, for all crime. Clearly, such a discourse cannot be explained merely by poverty or by a supposed hatred of the poor.

In Brazil, *aporophobia,* as a critical criminological concept, reflects a theoretical importation incompatible with the local reality of punitive power. This uncritical import carries the serious risk of reinforcing our already abyssally selective penal practices.

It is essential to construct criminological and penal knowledge that takes into account our peculiarities, historical scars, geopolitical subordination, and local epistemologies—especially those that use, as an interpretive key, our enduring slaveholding heritage.

The delegitimization of punitive power continues to be the most suitable path for critically and proactively confronting the marginal penal question in Brazil. In this light, *aporophobia* becomes a risk, not a remedy, as it promotes a re-legitimization of that same power.

Far from escaping juridical-penal idealism, *aporophobia* emerges precisely from it. Though cloaked in critical language, it ultimately reinforces the very system it claims to critique through a near-theological faith in the supposed virtues of criminal law.

The attempt to construct a criminological critique around *aporophobia*—with its simplified diagnosis of an alleged aversion to the poor—marks the rise of a brand-new punitive left. In order to avoid being labeled punitivist, it appeals to penal aggravations, which, even when not constituting new types, open new fields of selectivity in the lived world.

The legislative initiatives proposing to classify *aporophobia* as a qualifying circumstance in homicide, bodily harm, and insult reflect a complete absence of critical analysis in criminal lawmaking. These initiatives are rooted in symbolic criminal law and are detached from any realistic penal, criminological, or legislative perspective.

The theoretical, methodological, and, consequently, political positions offered by intersectionality and Southern epistemologies provide valuable heuristic tools for understanding, with completeness—although without abandoning specificities—the structure and function of punitive power. These approaches also help to expose the inadequacies of *aporophobia* as a critical concept in criminology, particularly its lack of interdisciplinarity and its detachment from local social realities.

GPSR Compliance

The European Union's (EU) General Product Safety Regulation (GPSR) is a set of rules that requires consumer products to be safe and our obligations to ensure this.

If you have any concerns about our products, you can contact us on ProductSafety@springernature.com

In case Publisher is established outside the EU, the EU authorized representative is:

Springer Nature Customer Service Center GmbH
Europaplatz 3
69115 Heidelberg, Germany

Batch number: 09013046

Printed by Printforce, the Netherlands